Leadership and Communication

Jon-Arild Johannessen

Leadership and Communication

Concepts, Contexts, and Tools

palgrave
macmillan

Jon-Arild Johannessen
Kristiania University College
Holstebro, Denmark

ISBN 978-3-031-40847-2 ISBN 978-3-031-40848-9 (eBook)
https://doi.org/10.1007/978-3-031-40848-9

Cover illustration: VLADGRIN

This Palgrave Macmillan imprint is published by the registered company Springer Nature Switzerland AG
The registered company address is: Gewerbestrasse 11, 6330 Cham, Switzerland

Paper in this product is recyclable.

Preface

In this book, we use the term leadership to refer to management, control and communication in social systems. The leadership perspective is related to information processes, visions, objectives, deviations and the re-establishment of the system's course. In this book, we define communication by means of the following statement: Who says what to whom, through which channels and with what effect? Moreover, we describe, analyse and explore in depth the place of communication in leadership.

A manager uses a great deal of time on communication, was one of the findings in Henry Mintzberg's 1973 book *The Nature of Managerial Work*. A follow-up study 30 years later found that aspects of Mintzberg's findings concerning managerial work were no longer relevant, but the level of communication had not diminished to any appreciable extent.

We also use Mintzberg's term case letters to exemplify some points in a description, analysis or to bring out a practical perspective. Case letter is a term Mintzberg uses for short reports, analyses and discussion of organizations, but which cannot be considered a full-fledged case study. Case letters can be understood as a case example, where you show different sides of a problem, a problem statement or a research question. A case letter elaborates on some aspects of a problem that you want to have illuminated from a certain point of view.

With regard to a leader's communications, it seems reasonable to say that information is the 'glue' that holds communication together. However, if too much 'glue' is used, the consequence is information overload, which hampers effective communication. If there is too little glue, individuals and entire organizations may find themselves in a pathological state of disorder, with people filling the information vacuum with rumours and gossip. Leadership communication can be involving and participatory, motivating colleagues to be creative and put in as much extra effort as is necessary. Leadership communication can also be power-based and patronizing. Such a style of communication will cause tensions and conflicts within an organization.

In this book, we are interested in information and communication as part of a special type of interaction, namely situations where one wants to generate trust or influence.

We have developed 26 case letters (case examples) and 17 practical exercises in Part I of the book. These case letters and exercises are directly linked to the topics in the respective chapters. Both case letters and exercises are developed so that the reader (student) can deepen their understanding of the concepts and contexts that are elaborated in the chapter.

In Part II, we develop six personal communication tools, and six personal coaching tools, with assignment to each of the coaching tools. In addition, we have developed 66 exercises to the six personal communication tools.

Holstebro, Denmark

Jon-Arild Johannessen
Kristiania University College

Contents

List of Figures

Part I

Communication in Leadership-Processes

Communication and Leadership 1

Aims of this Chapter

Understanding the concepts: influencing, information, conflict, messages

Everyday Leadership Communication

Most of us experience daily situations where we communicate with other people with the aim of achieving a specific goal. Obviously, this is only one part of the communication process, but for many people it is an important part, and for most of us it can be a crucial part in certain situations (Foster et al. 2019). One example of a way of influencing other people, which is discussed in this book, is illustrated in the following case letter.

Case Letter: Ignorance Seems to Be Institutionalized

A student queueing to use the photocopier asks: 'Excuse me, could I go to the front of the queue? It's because I need to get to a lecture'. This approach achieved a positive response 94 per cent of the time in several experiments. If the 'because' sentence was omitted, the positive response rate fell to 60%. If a 'because' sentence was included, but provided only nonsensical information, then the positive response rate was 93%. For example: 'Excuse me, could I go to the front of the queue? It's because I need to do some copying'. At first sight this makes no sense, because it seems reasonable to assume that everyone in the queue is there because

K. Ledingham et al., *Rethinking Innovation*,
https://doi.org/10.1007/978-3-031-40848-9_1

they need to do some copying. However, the explanation lies in the word **because,** which seems to trigger a cognitive reflex in most people.[1]

Communication—Conflict and Interpretation

We all experience situations where another party does not understand the information we wanted to communicate in the way we would have wanted them to understand it. In such situations, conflicts can easily arise. Conflicts can also arise easily when the other party interprets something we say in a way completely different to our intended meaning. Our emotions get involved and the ensuing unavoidable conflict can easily get out of control. This happens in family situations, in organizations and in wider society.

The ways in which we communicate with others and the concepts and words we use are also significant for our own sense of identity and that of the person we are communicating with. An example of this, which we discuss in this book, is how we create a social reality, as shown in the following case letter.

Case Letter: Being Illiterate Is Not the Same as Not Being Able to Read

The word illiteracy denotes an inability to read or write. This is the meaning we have assigned to this word. If we consider this concept at face value, it is an objective social fact that some countries have higher levels of illiteracy than others. Perhaps it is also an ordinary social phenomenon that increased industrialization reduces the level of illiteracy in a country. However, we can also incorporate a wider meaning into the concept of illiteracy: For example, if large part of a country's population can read and write, but have difficulties comprehending the meaning and context of what they read and write, we could describe this situation by extending the concept of illiteracy to make it broader than is usually the case. We could say that some people are functionally illiterate, even though they can read and write.

Information and Messages

In many settings, we are interested in disseminating the information we possess to others, in such a way that it is understood and accepted. In this way, we can establish cooperation and perform certain activities more effectively. An example of this, which we discuss in this book, is shown in the following case letter.

[1] https://www.psychologytoday.com/intl/blog/brain-wise/201310/the-power-the-word-because-get-people-do-stuff.

Case Letter: We Change Our Opinion When We Get New Information

Two people have a disagreement about how to share an apple. They agree to divide it into two equal parts. Person A uses their half to make freshly pressed juice, throwing away the leftover pulp. Person B presses their half to get rid of the juice, using the pulp to make a cake. If A and B had clarified their objectives in advance (or during the communication process), both would have benefited from a variation on the apparently fair solution of dividing the apple equally.

Hope Is a Waking Dream

It can be difficult to accept the existence of certain techniques that function better than others in processes involving the communication of information, such that insight into these techniques gives one party an advantage over the other. Such techniques have been known and used since antiquity, however (Bouty & Drucker-Godard 2018). This book examines some of these techniques. Insight into these techniques can help not only with the presentation of one's own message, but also with getting an accurate understanding of the other party's presentation. Used responsibly, we believe that insight into some of these techniques can contribute to correcting bias in any communication. Used irresponsibly, insight into some of these techniques can be exploited in power games that may ultimately escalate conflict and fail to promote genuine communication.

Communication is a phenomenon that is part of our everyday lives, ranging from the personal to the local, regional and international levels. We communicate with each other in diverse contexts, such as entering into and dissolving marriages and cohabiting relationships, having conflicts over budgets, neighbour quarrels over fences, negotiations about fishing rights in international waters, conflicts between nations, and in everyday activities, such as the buying and selling of goods and services.

We wish to examine and discuss the functions that are involved in any act of communication. However, our particular focus will be on the importance of information and communication for leaders in their everyday working lives. Our aim is to uncover the processes that, once linked together, form the pattern from which we can study any act of communication.

Exercises

Take the seven questions below as the basis for a group discussion. Discuss each question in order to arrive at some answers. Write down your answers. When you have finished reading the whole of this book, return to these questions, discuss them again and write down your answers. Now compare these answers with your original answers, and discuss the differences.

1. Why do we trust one type of information more than another?
2. Why do we have more confidence in what one person tells us than in what another person tells us?
3. How can we use information and communication to generate trust?
4. How can we use information and communication to influence other people?
5. How is communication affected by how we demarcate the boundaries of a problem?
6. What information processes operate in communication situations?
7. How does the framing of a situation affect the situation regarding communication?

References

Bouty, I. & Drucker-Godard, C. (2018). Managerial work and coordination: A practice-based approach on board a racing sailboat. Human Relations, 72, 3: 565–587.

Foster, W.M., Hassard, J.S., Morris, J. & Wolfram, J. (2019). The changing nature of managerial work: The effects of corporate restructuring on management jobs and careers. Human Relations, 72, 3:473–504.

Communication and Metaphors

2

Aims of this Chapter

1. To generate a discussion on the concept of roles
2. In this chapter, the reader should reflect on the following concepts:
   Differences, relationships, processes, patterns, contexts, symmetrical relationships, complementary relationships, linear processes, circular processes, positive feedback loop dominance, negative feedback loop dominance.

Metaphors

Life is not a theatre, but if we define it as a theatre, it will become like a theatrical performance as a consequence. The point of this statement is that it is doubtful whether the metaphor of a theatre gives any insight at all into communications processes. With this hypothesis, we distance ourselves from the concept of using 'roles' and other theatrical metaphors (Dowell et al. 2018: 1007–1041; Johannessen 2018, 2020).

Obviously, roles do exist outside theatrical and similar settings. The fact that we employ the concept of a role *metaphorically* is a completely different matter. But confusing a metaphor with reality is the same as confusing a map with the actual terrain. The extent to which roles and other theatrical metaphors are enlightening or revealing in relation to communication is obviously open to discussion. In this book, our approach is that using theatrical metaphors in relation to communication tends to obscure rather than enlighten. In theatrical metaphors, life is viewed as a drama that we are acting out, with us all performing different roles in different acts. However, people often confuse metaphors with reality. In everyday language we often hear: 'the mother's role', rather than 'the role as mother', or 'the boss's role', rather than 'the role as boss'. This distinction is crucial for understanding

K. Ledingham et al., *Rethinking Innovation*,
https://doi.org/10.1007/978-3-031-40848-9_2

the distinction between metaphor and reality. Largely, we have drifted from using theatrical metaphors as metaphors towards seeing roles, actors and so on as a part of real life. But there can be no doubt that no sane person would think of taking a walk on a map and using the terrain to orient themselves. In a way, the distinction between metaphor and reality is removed by the concept of roles, among other things. To a large extent what happens is that we create models for reality, rather than models of reality. When we create models for reality, and use the concept of roles, for example, then life really does become a theatre that is played out in different acts. In psychiatry, this is called a psychotic break with reality and in the most extreme cases a schizophrenic person might eat a menu because the word 'fish' is printed on it (Watzlawick 1984, 1988).

Consequently, we will avoid the metaphor of the 'role' and other metaphors drawn from the theatre, because we believe they too readily have a tendency to be confused with reality and be perceived as real elements. Instead, we will use concepts that we believe can help in our understanding of information and communication processes. The main concepts we will use to describe and analyse communication are: **differences, distinctions, relationships, processes, patterns** and **context**. These are concepts that attempt to reveal the genuine form of communication, as opposed to metaphors drawn from the world of physics such as power (force) and energy (Bateson 1972; Bunge 1996, 1998, 1999, Johannessen 2020a).

Just as energy, force and momentum are fundamental concepts both in physics, and in the study of the physical world, the concepts of differences, distinctions, relationships, processes, patterns and context are fundamental to the study of information and communication.

This book is structured around the conceptual model shown in Fig. 2.1.

Communication, credibility and influence are important elements, because of the increasing mobility in today's society (Peticca-Harris 2018; Johannessen 2021a, 2022). This also leads to major organizational restructuring that demands effective communication. The emergence of the innovation economy in the Fourth Industrial Revolution also explains why we today have to deal with continually increasing information (Schwab 2017). In order to convey and interpret this information, communication is an essential prerequisite.

Information and communication form an essential part of the mechanisms used to resolve conflicts. Information here means the communicable part of knowledge that is conveyed to others and understood by them. Communication facilitates a common understanding of the world. At the same time, communication can also establish new knowledge when two or more people share and contribute their experiences by communicating these as information in a social process (Holm-Pedersen et al. 2018).

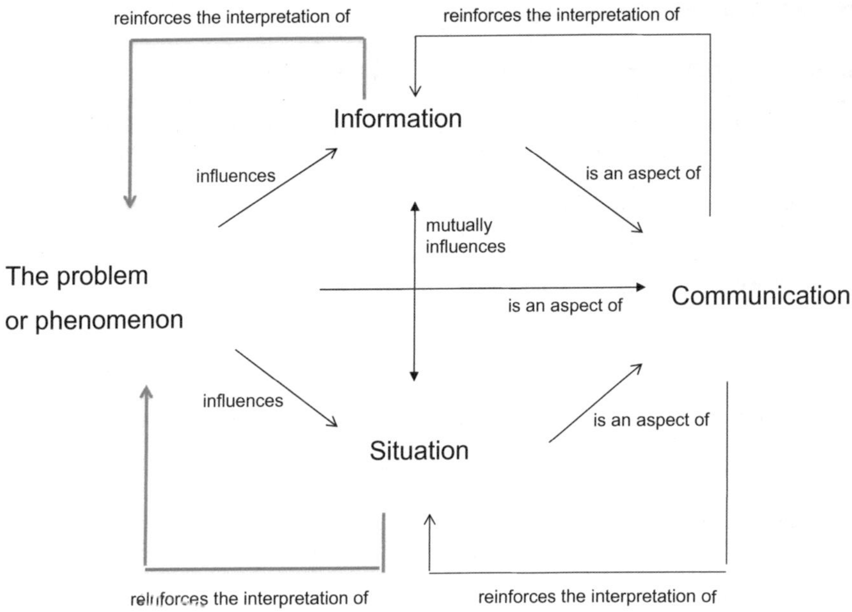

Fig. 2.1 Communication

Exercises

1. Discuss the following statement: Everything is seen, heard and said by a subject, and accordingly is subjective.
2. Take as your starting point a conflict you experienced recently with a close friend. Try to go through the communication that took place and answer the following questions:
   a) What was the main disagreement that emerged in the conflict?
   b) How did your relationship change as the conflict grew in intensity?
   c) In what way would you say that the communication between you focused on pointing out whatever was the cause of the conflict?
   d) Try to describe the pattern that evolved: Is it possible to identify any features of your interaction that tended to recur frequently?
   e) How would you characterize the conclusion of the conflict? Was it the case that one party won and the other lost? Or did both of you feel that you had won? Or were there other contexts that emerged?

References

Bateson,G. (1972). Steps to an ecology of mind, Intex Books, London.
Bunge, M. (1996). Finding philosophy in social science, New Haven CT: Yale University Press
Bunge, M. (1998). Social science under debate, University of Toronto Press, Toronto.
Bunge, M. (1999). The sociology-philosophy connection, Transaction Publishers, New Brunswick, NJ.
Dowell, N.M.M., Nixon, T.M. & Graesser, A.C. (2018). Group communication analysis. Behaviour Research Methods, 51, 3: 1007–1041.
Johannessen, J-A. (2018). Innovation leads to economic crises, Palgrave, London.
Johannessen, J-A. (2020). The workplace of the future, Routledge, London.
Johannessen, J-A. (2020a). Automation, innovation and economic crises: Survival the fourth industrial revolution, Routledge, London.
Johannessen, J-A. (2021a). Artificial intelligence, automation and ethics in the innovation economy, Routledge, London.
Johannessen, J-A. (2022). Creativity, innovation and the fourth industrial revolution: The da Vinci strategy, Routledge, London.
Peticca-Harris, A. (2018). Managing compassionately? Managerial narratives about grief and compassion. Human Relations, 72, 3: 588–612.
Schwab, K. (2017). The fourth industrial revolution, Portfolio Penguin, New York.
Watzlawick, P. (1984). The invented reality: How do we know what we believe we know? W.W. Norton & Company, London.
Watzlawick, P. (1988). Ultra Solutions: How to fail most successfully, W.W. Norton & Company, New York.

Requisite Variety

3

Aims in this Chapter

1. This chapter is designed to give the reader an understanding of how the way a problem is framed is crucial for how it is perceived, both by the recipient of a message and the person who wants to convey a message.
2. In this chapter, the reader should reflect on the following concepts:

   Systemic structuring, the displaced error, the communicable part of knowledge, tacit knowledge, hidden knowledge, analogy, dualistic conceptual pairs, psychological Maginot lines.

When You Don't Greet a Colleague, You Objectify Him or Her

How we structure a problem is crucial in a situation involving communication, because it gives meaning to the situation we find ourselves in. The point of organizing a problem in this fashion is to gain an overview of the boundaries we ought to set, the context the problem is part of, the relationship between the problem's parts and whole (systemic structuring) and the different perspectives of the parties on the problem.

Our view of the world influences how we structure a problem. In other words, it is important to be aware of the fact that as observers, we are part of the social environment, and thus influence the situation by the way we structure a problem. Consequently, we are not external to the problem we are observing and examining. In communication situations, as in other types of social interaction, we are always part of what we observe. It is important to be aware of this distinction. We are not mere 'objective' observers of a social reality. We are part of what we observe, and this makes problem-structuring extremely difficult. If we are not aware of this, then we will often find ourselves in a situation that conflicts with our expectations

K. Ledingham et al., *Rethinking Innovation*,
https://doi.org/10.1007/978-3-031-40848-9_3

regarding what we think we should observe. One cannot create a social reality in the same way as a carpenter makes a table. We are part of what is created and we are thus changed in this process. There is a mutual interaction between us, as observers of the social reality, and the social reality itself (Johannessen, 2020b, 2022b).

The communication situation will always be the total situation of which a problem is part. Although an individual deals with a series or group of problems, these will all be included in the actors' consciousness, as in a total situation.

Any problem in a communication situation may be viewed as being framed by a boundary line to other problems—problems that may be regarded as being collectively part of an overall communication situation. How we structure a problem and where we set the boundaries of the problem thus affect the overall situation. Bateson (1972: 292–293) terms this 'punctuation'. Through the process of punctuation, events are punctuated in a certain way to attribute causality. By creating linear causality that does not necessarily exist in the real world, one is then free to discuss cause and effect. A sequence of a process is selected, and then bracketed. In this way, we separate what is punctuated from the rest of the process. Figuratively, we may imagine this as a circle that is divided into small pieces; one piece of the circle is then selected and folded out into a straight line. This results in the creation of an artificial beginning and end. This beginning and end of course cannot exist in a circle, but only through the process of punctuation

If we wish to explain a communication process, it is not sufficient to consider the individual components separately that the process consists of, and then summarize the results. The explanation must be based on considering the whole system of communication; generally, the result will be quite different from the sum of the individual results (Bunge 1997: 414; Johannessen 2022d, 2023c).

The opposite approach, in which one summarizes the individual parts in order to reach a final result, may be understood as a 'displaced error'.

Case Letter: Guinea Fowl Logic

A displaced error is like crushing nuts to collect data on the shape of cracks, or collecting sawdust to make a complete tree. There is little point in using resources to solve problems that get eliminated along the way or that change when they are put into a real context. In a way, this is like using a lot of resources to solve problems that don't exist in the social context, even though they allow themselves to be solved very successfully in well-designed models.

Waving People Away as Though They Were Flies

To completely understand a communication situation, we must understand the cultural expressions that the parties use and, not least, the expressions we use ourselves. The latter is not easy, as it is always difficult for us to evaluate what we

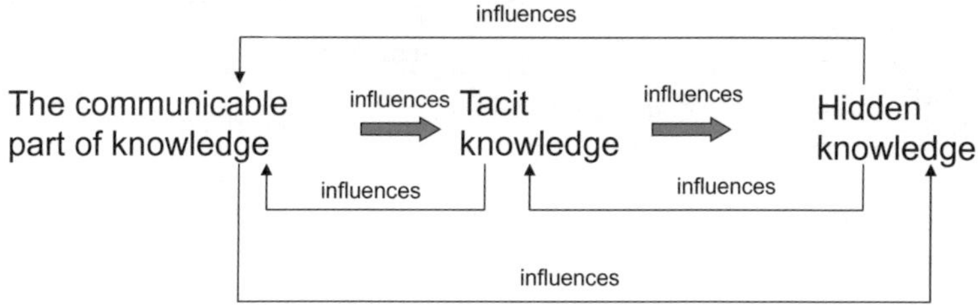

Fig. 3.1 Structuring knowledge

are doing wrong ourselves, because we adhere to fixed behavioural patterns. It is relatively simple to observe differences and changes, but more difficult to observe cultural expressions which are more constant and taken for granted. We need to make it clear to ourselves how we communicate our own cultural expressions. A conflict may easily occur and get out of control, if we are not aware of how we are perceived by the other party. One way to do this consciously is to make it quite clear to ourselves what cultural expressions we are using in a communication process.

Another point in problem-structuring is that knowledge is woven together like a cloth, so that each part of the knowledge only becomes meaningful when it is put into context with the other parts.

One approach to structuring knowledge is shown in Fig. 3.1.

The communicable part of knowledge is the part of the knowledge that can be communicated to others as information, verbal and non-verbal. In this way, information, knowledge and communication are linked together in a close system.

Tacit knowledge, says Polanyi (1958), is the type of knowledge related to our skills that it is difficult to convey to others by using language; for instance, teaching someone how to ride a bicycle (Schøn 1983, 1987).

Hidden knowledge is here defined as the type of knowledge that structures our premises, assumptions, prerequisites and motives. In other words, the fact that this type of knowledge is 'hidden' makes it difficult for us to gain insight into what guides our actions and attitudes, such as our attitudes towards people from foreign cultures. If this knowledge remains more or less hidden from our consciousness, conflicts may easily arise without us knowing why or how they are created.

Dialogue between people will make parts of the tacit and hidden knowledge accessible within the communicable part of the knowledge we are conveying, and can thus be used as information. If this does not occur, then when we are structuring a problem, we will not be fully aware of how our hidden knowledge can influence the problem-structuring, and the problem-structuring may thus end up with a different design and result than if we were aware of the hidden knowledge (Johannessen 2023, 2023a).

One method that can be used when structuring a problem is to divide the problem into its main logical elements; in the case of an economic model, this could be done by examining the elements of production and consumption (the main logical

Main logical elements / Analytical concepts	Problem area	
	Main logical element A	Main logical element B
Concept A	Possible / probable	Possible / probable
Concept B	Possible / probable	Possible / probable
Concept C	Possible / probable	Possible / probable

Fig. 3.2 Problem-structuring matrix

elements in Fig. 3.2). These main logical elements can then be placed in a matrix on a horizontal axis. Along the vertical axis of the matrix, we can then insert the analytical concepts used, such as labour, capital and resources. In order to study the overall problem, the next step would be to consider each analytical concept in relation to the cells located on the right side of the analytical concept. If all the cells become meaningful, one will then be assured that the analytical concepts have some durability. The same approach may also be applied when using analogies to see if the analogies and concepts are at the same logical level (Johannessen 2023b).

However, if we use analogies in problem-structuring in order to make a point, then we should not make the mistake of using analogies at a different logical level. For instance, one rhetorical stratagem is to use analogies at a different logical level than the problem at hand, in order to confuse the other party. For example, in a debate about how to manage a nation's finances, it would be erroneous to use a household analogy of 'living within one's means'; this would be a so-called category error. Such a rhetorical stratagem is often used in communication to confuse the other party.

The Difference that Makes the Difference

An extension of the approach described above is to start with vague concepts and analogies, and then to test these out in a problem-structuring matrix. If this does not provide a solution that makes sense, then we should amend our analytical concepts and re-run the test to see if they withstand the matrix test. The point of this approach is that we avoid becoming too set initially in the concepts and analogies we are using to analyse the problem.

We have an unfortunate tendency to use dualistic concepts unthinkingly, such as radical-conservative, evil-good, true–false, where, in many contexts, these serve to obscure rather than clarify the phenomenon about which something is being said. For example, if we say in a discussion that the opposite of 'free / freedom' is unfreedom or enslavement, then this sounds plausible at first sight. However, in some contexts, the opposite of 'free' is not enslavement but solidarity (for example, 'free' trade as opposed to 'fair' trade).

If we build up large parts of our analytical conceptual framework by using such dualistic conceptual pairs, an analytical pattern may be established that does not necessarily correspond to the phenomenon we want to know more about. This may be compared to wearing blue-tinted glasses in order to study blue colours in nature. This metaphor is perhaps not the most appropriate to illustrate this problem, because wearing blue-tinted glasses will only have consequences for oneself, whereas using incongruous analytical concepts in a communication situation can have disastrous consequences for others (Johannessen, 2023e).

One phenomenon that we often overlook in problem-structuring is the paradox that we often don't know what the real problem is until we look at its possible consequences or solutions. One method is to tread carefully and use the problem-structuring matrix, and thoroughly reflect upon the suitability of the analytical concepts before formalizing them.[1]

If we do not spend enough time on problem-structuring, we can end up building a psychological Maginot Line[2] which may seem to be solid and defensible, but which is breached in the first 'attack'.

If the problem is structured incorrectly, and we then design models based on this, the actions we take based on these models will also be incorrect. Incorrect structuring of a problem may stem, among other things, from setting the boundaries of a problem too narrowly. In any problem-complex, there will always be innumerable facts. When we select some facts and discard other facts, these may turn out to be the facts that were the essential ones. That is, the facts selected may not be the most important facts, resulting in the actions based on the models we develop then being incorrect. When we find relationships in the model that are difficult to identify in the real world, we must be aware that experiences are always different from what was experienced, in the same way that a description is always different from what is described, or more specifically that there is a difference between a map and the terrain.

In social contexts, it is the expectation that something will happen that often triggers what actually happens, and consequently it is also important how we structure a problem. We seem to have a tendency to think in terms of linear cause and

[1] Reflections on problem-structuring matrixes can be found in Bateson's book *Steps to an Ecology of Mind* (1972).

[2] The Maginot Line was a line of French fortifications, which was deemed impenetrable, but which was easily breached by the Germans during the initial phase of World War II.

effect in our social lives, whereas in reality circular causal explanations using feedback loops are often more appropriate. One consequence of thinking in linear causal models is that we often cause more problems when trying to solve a problem.

Exercises

1. Discuss what you think is meant by the following statements:
   a) Splitting an egg into half to get two chickens.
   b) We cannot study time by taking apart a clock.
2. List five points that are crucial to pay attention to if you want to positively influence someone from a foreign culture.
3. Try to clarify how you think when you are going to write a note aimed at influencing the leader of the department. Remember, it is not *what* you think, but *how* you think that should be clarified.
4. Give some examples of tacit knowledge.
5. Give some examples of hidden knowledge.
6. How can hidden knowledge guide our actions?
7. How can the models we use have a detrimental effect on others?
8. Why do we select some facts and not others when we want to communicate something to others?
9. What is meant by the statements:
   a) Experiences are different from what is experienced.
   b) The description is different from what is described.
10. What is meant by the statement, 'it is the expectation that something will happen that creates actions?'.
11. What is meant by the statement, 'as observers of social reality, we are always part of this reality?'.
12. What is meant by the statement, 'often we do not know what the real problem is until we look at its possible consequences or solutions?'.
13. Give four examples of psychological Maginot lines.

References

Bateson, G. (1972). Steps to an ecology of mind, Intex Books, London.

Bunge, M. (1997). Mechanism and explanation. Philosophy of the Social Sciences 27: 410–465.

Johannessen, J-A. (2020b). Artificial intelligence, automation and the future of competence at work, Routledge.

Johannessen, J-A. (2022b). The philosophy of tacit knowledge, Emerald, London.

Johannessen, J-A. (2022d). Intelligent robots consciousness and creativity: The search for hidden knowledge, the cognitive side of knowledge management, Emerald, London.

Johannessen, J-A. (2023). A Marxist interpretation of Church leadership: Romans: 13: 1–7. Lexington Books, New York.

Johannessen, J-A. (2023a). Feudal capitalism: The political economy of the innovation society, Routledge, London.
Johannessen, J-A. (2023b). De-globalization, China-US tensions in the Innovation Economy, Routledge, London.
Johannessen, J-A. (2023c). Artificial intelligence and creativity: Implications for automation in the innovation economy, Routledge, London.
Johannessen, J-A. (2023e). Aspects of a theory of genocide, Trivent Publishong, London.
Polanyi, M. (1958). Personal knowledge, Routledge & Kegan Paul, London.
Schøn, D. (1983). The reflective practitioner. How professionals think in action, Basic Books, New York.
Schøn, D. (1987). Educating the reflective practitioner, Jossey-Bass, London

Where We Draw the Boundaries of a Problem Affects Our Perception of the Problem

4

Aims of this Chapter

1. To provide insight into how setting an overly narrow boundary can give a message a specific meaning, while setting a wider boundary can give a completely different meaning.
2. In this chapter, the reader should reflect on the following concepts:
   Patterns, symmetrical relationships, complementary relationships.

Contexts Create Meaning

A phenomenon that is separated from its context by setting overly narrow boundaries can lead to completely different results than if the boundaries were not so narrow (Kidron and Vinarski-Peretz, 2018). It is the *relationships* between various elements that can give us an understanding of the phenomenon/problem about which we are trying to say something. The case letter below attempts to illustrate the consequences of setting boundaries that are too narrow or wide, and the importance of the relationships between the elements of a phenomenon.

Case Letter: Patterns

The birds flying above a certain spot on the Bird Island Fjord indicate that there are fish just below the surface of the water. Interpreted by an experienced fisherman, this pattern indicates what kind of fish they are, what size and how deep they are in the ocean.

K. Ledingham et al., *Rethinking Innovation*,
https://doi.org/10.1007/978-3-031-40848-9_4

Relevant Relationships

If the relevant relationships forming a pattern are broken, the information we create may be of little use to an observer. Use of this information may also be directly harmful to those affected by the consequences of the actions based on the information.

It is the patterns tying together the whole horizon of understanding that will be of interest. However, in certain contexts, as researchers, we do not really know what we are looking for until we find it; consequently, in such cases, fragmentation and cutting away of relevant relationships could be disastrous. We may risk focusing only on the indicators (the birds in the above example), and not on what is of interest, what we really are looking for (the fish in the above example). Breaking up relevant patterns may cause the crucial relationships to be lost to us as observers.

It is the pattern within which the information is included on which we must constantly focus, rather than on the single elements in an event or action. The special characteristic of a pattern is that it is difficult to point out cause and effect. A pattern may be considered metaphorically as a circle, and in a circle there is no beginning or end.

We should always demarcate a problem in accordance with our objectives, i.e. if we are seeking answers to one particular question, then the boundaries will be different than if we seek answers to a different question, even if it is related to the same phenomenon or problem.

Case Letter: Setting Boundaries

Ms Hansen had a problem with constantly watering eyes. If a neurologist were to examine her problem, he would probably restrict his examination to a physical examination of Ms Hansen's body, and more narrowly to her tear ducts. However, a psychoanalyst examining Ms Hansen might set boundaries around the problem by looking into her childhood. Looking at the same problem, a communication specialist might want to find out the pattern of relationships that Ms Hansen has entered into and set boundaries for these. Of course, this is just a hypothetical scenario; the most sensible thing would probably be to start off by asking Ms Hansen what she thought was the cause of the problem. The idea of this example is to point out that the boundaries of a problem are always related to our purpose or of what we want to gain an understanding.

Setting the Boundaries of a Problem Is No Trivial Matter

The issue of where we set the boundaries of a problem is no trivial matter. It is absolutely crucial for the outcome we arrive at concerning the question we asked, even if we were all to pose the same question about the same phenomenon or problem. To set the correct boundaries, the following question may be asked: What elements of the problem are relevant to understanding the situation?

The above can be expressed by the following two sentences:

1. The way in which a problem is structured provides many of the premises for the actual solution.
2. Our assumptions about the demarcation of a problem will often restrict our choices about how to deal with it, and creative solutions almost always lie outside conventional assumptions.

Boundary Problem

One type of boundary problem that we often encounter in a communication context is whether we should solve one problem at a time, or view all the problems together.

In groups where basic relationships are a mixture of collaboration and competition, the use of the agenda principle (solving one problem at a time) will be less effective than if no agenda is used (Johannessen, 2022).

The alternative is to discuss all the problems together and consider how best they can be integrated. The procedure using such an approach is as follows:

1. Identify which problems to prioritize.
2. Uncover individual interests.
3. Develop suggestions for creative approaches to solve the problem.

Structuring of group negotiations can be organized according to decision-making rules and how the agenda is structured. Decision-making rules in group negotiations can be divided into the majority principle, i.e. a majority vote; and into a principle of consensus, which here means that the parties have to reach a compromise within a given deadline.

The agenda can be organized so that you discuss points case by case or instead by simultaneous discussions, i.e. so that you can address a problem that is not necessarily related to a particular item on the agenda.

Figure 4.1 provides an overview of how group negotiations can be structured.

The extent to which mixed groups should make decisions by simple majority or by consensus depends on the results one wants to achieve.

'Agenda' organization / Decision-making rules	Case for case	Simultaneous discussions
Simple majority	Collaborative groups	Mixed groups
Consensus	Adversarial groups	Mixed groups

Fig. 4.1 Structure of group negotiations

Case Letter: What Is Our Goal?

If we are looking for creative solutions, then consensus is probably the most rational decision-making approach. If a group is under strong pressure to make a decision quickly, then it is probably better to use majority voting.

Purely adversarial groups, i.e. groups characterized by extreme competitiveness and mutual distrust (a symmetrical relationship), and collaborative groups, i.e. groups characterized by a basically helpful attitude and mutual trust (complementary relationship), will probably benefit from solving complex problems on a case-by-case basis.

If adversarial groups opt for consensus-based decision-making, they will be forced to reach a compromise. They will then be obliged to implement their compromise decision at a later date precisely because they were personally involved in reaching it.

As a general rule, collaborative groups will be inclined to comply with whatever decisions are made, and accordingly will save time by using majority voting.

When groups use majority voting, however, it can easily result in the quest for votes being prioritized over the quest for information. This can reduce opportunities for making the best decisions for the system as a whole.

It can be advantageous to put easy problems at the start of the agenda, however, as success solving these problems may give the group momentum for further success. Researchers have found that this approach is more likely to produce situations where both parties are winners (win–win situations).

Exercises

1. Discuss the following statements:
   a) When the cause is identified, the effect has always occurred already.
   b) Predictions made with hindsight are almost always correct.
2. Take a familiar problem as your starting point. What are the main elements of the problem? Discuss whether you all agree on the choice of main elements.

3. Discuss the following statements:
   a) The way in which a problem is structured provides many of the premises for the actual solution.
   b) Our assumptions about the demarcation of a problem will often restrict our choices about how to deal with it, and creative solutions almost always lie outside conventional assumptions.
4. What is the meaning of this statement, 'we should always demarcate a problem in accordance with our objectives, or with what we are trying to understand?'
   a) Give at least three examples that shed light on this statement.

References

Johannessen, J-A. (2022). Creativity, innovation and the fourth industrial revolution: The da Vinci strategy, Routledge, London.

Kidron, A. & Vinarski-Peretz, H. (2018). The political iceberg: the hidden side of leaders' political behaviour. Leadership & Organization Development Journal, 39, 8:1010–1023.

The Context Sends Messages

5

Aims of this Chapter

1. To provide an insight into why a communication situation can be perceived differently depending on which psychological framework we choose to use.
2. In this chapter, the reader should reflect on the following concepts:
   Context, win–win, win-lose, ambiguity, mental model, point of reference.

The Context Influences the Action

A phenomenon or problem will be difficult to understand if the parties involved do not have the same understanding of the context. A simple example of the context providing the framework that determines how something is understood is shown in the case letter below.

Case Letter: The Context Guides Behaviour

The symbol ‘O’ can refer to the digit ‘O’ or the letter ‘O’. What the symbol refers to will be unclear unless we know the context in which it is used:

1. SON
2. 1O1

Both 1 and 2 above contain the symbol ‘O’, but have different meanings because of the different contexts.

K. Ledingham et al., *Rethinking Innovation*,
https://doi.org/10.1007/978-3-031-40848-9_5

Understanding the context is crucial for mastering the most elementary activities in social situations. The context is only relevant to us if we understand what it is trying to say.

Two dogs playing look as though they are about to tear each other's throats out, but they are actually playing. They have an understanding of the context: 'we're playing'. Consequently, the context determines that the dogs will come to no harm. However, if the context signalled that this was a fight for food or survival, then their behaviour would be completely different, as well as the consequences—then they would perhaps really tear out each other's throats! In this way, it might be said that even animals have an understanding of different contexts.

The Context Constitutes the Psychological Framework

The context can be perceived as the psychological framework that guides our behaviour and actions in situations. On the other hand, it never determines our actions; it only functions as a guide to how our scope of action is perceived, and thus provides a guide for our behaviour. Context can be compared to the concept of culture. A specific culture only becomes visible when expressed through patterns of behaviour in society. This is similar to context. The context only becomes visible through its modes of expression in practical situations (Bateson 1972: 162–166).

Context must not be confused with the physical environment. Context has nothing to do with physical aspects. It is a psychological element, or, if you will, a mental framework that controls our way of thinking and acting in certain situations. Any context will also form part of a larger context, which in turn will guide behaviour in the smaller contexts (the first context). In communication situations, it is crucial that we are aware of this (Luhmann 1996).

Case Letter: Facts have a Greater Impact than the Truth

A negotiation situation between a Japanese and a European firm regarding the development of a fibre optic product provided the following context hierarchy:

1. This is trade.
2. Eastern and Western ways of thinking.

The results of the negotiation situation will depend on our being aware of this distinction between contexts, and at the same time the content of the two contexts. In order to clarify contexts, the following applies:

1. Distinguish between context types and
2. Be familiar with the contexts, i.e. the content of the context.

If the Soup You Are Served Tastes Bad, Complain to the Cookbook Publisher

A solution in negotiations is said to be integrative or win–win, when the different interests of the parties are reorganized in such a way that both gain benefits (Arden 2015).

Integrative solutions are important because they promote long-term stability in relations between parties and improve organizational efficiency.

Integrative solutions can be said to exist at a higher level than compromises. Compromises are simple solutions whereby differences in the distances between the parties (the negotiating zone) are subdivided.

Case Letter: Integrative Solutions

Person A wants the window to be open to get fresh air. Person B wants the window closed because of noise from the street. Compromise: The window is open for half of every day. Integrative solution: A ventilation system is installed.

When the Realities Change, I Change My Opinion

When we change the context of a communication situation from win-lose to win–win, the result is that the meaning we assigned to the situation has changed. Our point here is that we assign meanings to situations. The facts of the situation have not changed, but when we assign a different meaning to a situation, then consequentially the situation will change for us, and herein lies the whole point of framing a communications situation such that it appears as a win–win situation to the people involved.

In a win-lose situation, one side wins while the other loses. If it is a win–win situation, then the situation will be completely different for those involved, and a qualitatively different type of engagement and involvement will emerge.

What happens when we give a communication situation a qualitatively new meaning? Some will say that we have changed the objective reality by giving it a different meaning. Others will claim that we have created a new social reality in this process. The point is that by giving a communication situation a new meaning, the situation will appear differently to the actors involved. This meaning exists inside the minds of the actors, not in the objective world. However, the consequence is that the actors will relate to the communication situation in a qualitatively new way; that is, their actions and reactions will change.

Simply put, we can say that when we give a situation a new name, the word itself gives the situation a new meaning. The word takes on a reality, and therefore the words we use to denote a situation are crucial to the solutions we can create. We can say that the words we use to denote a situation set limits on the solutions we can create at a later point.

When a situation is given a new name, it will be difficult for the actors to understand that they could take actions that belonged to the action strategy of the situation when it had a different name. We have not only given the situation a new meaning (which is a mental activity), our physical actions have also become different as a result. In this way, a unity is created between the mental and the physical aspects, which is in contrast to the necessary distinction that normally exists between the two domains.

Case Letter: Names Mean Something

When we designate the Third World as 'underdeveloped', this then creates completely different associations and actions on our part than if we had designated these countries as 'undergoing an industrialization process'.

Concepts Have Consequences

When we notice that a communication situation changes when we give it a new name, our entire understanding of the situation changes as well. It will then be difficult to go back and look at the situation based on the mental map we previously used when considering the same situation. In other words, when we attribute a different meaning to a situation, the situation will also have changed in relation to the way the actors perceive it.

How should we proceed when changing a communication situation from a win-lose to a win–win situation? First, we should focus on the problem that has created the situation. The problem should be defined in such a way that it appears quite concrete. When this is done, we thoroughly review the solutions that have been attempted, and document what these solutions have led to in relation to the problem. Now that the problem has been described very clearly, and all the previous attempts at solutions are available, we can ask the simple question: What is needed to change the situation so that the problem is actually solved?

We first clarify the changes that need to be made in order to achieve a definitive solution to the problem. This should be done in a very concrete and detailed way. Then a plan should be drawn up to make the necessary changes.

The point of concretizing is to make sure that everyone can understand what is being said. Without such an understanding, it will be difficult to attribute new meaning to the situation. If the meaning is not fully understood, ambiguities may arise and new problems may be created, which will contribute to maintaining the original problem.

The Purpose of an Action Is Not Always Apparent Before the Action

It is often the case that mental models function in such a way that if the people involved in a communication situation have the feeling that they are 'winning', then they will feel that the others are 'losing', and vice versa. However, a communication situation is about more than just dividing up a given amount. An ideal communication situation will conclude with each of the parties feeling that they have gained something from being part of the process.

If a communication situation is based on the mental premise that the only way to win is if the other party loses, then in many cases both parties may lose.

Case Letter: Agree on the Objective

Two people have a disagreement about how to share an orange. They agree to divide it into two equal parts. One person uses their half to make freshly pressed juice, throwing away the leftover pulp. The other person presses their half to get rid of the juice, using the pulp to make a cake. If both parties had clarified their objectives in advance (or during the communication process), both would have benefited from a variation on the apparently fair solution of dividing the orange equally.

This is the same as the assumption that 'my interests' are not compatible with 'your interests', or: What is good for you must be bad for me. In order to create a win–win situation, it is important to clarify the objectives of the parties involved.

We can speak of a situation with high integrative potential (win–win situation, e.g. sharing an orange example above), with medium integrative potential (compromise context, e.g. car purchase and sale) and low integrative potential (win-lose situation, such as unconditional surrender at the end of a war). It is important that we always look for the best integrative potential of a problem.

However, in practice, it is very difficult to distinguish between competitive and collaborative contexts. When analysing and structuring a communication process, it is important to understand that the various parties often have mixed motives.

The Consequences of Structuring Win–Win Situations

The consequences of structuring a problem-complex as a win–win situation can be summarized as follows:

1. The conflicting interests of the parties can be changed so that their interests coincide.

   For example, instead of two countries increasing their defence spending with the aim of strengthening their security, economic cooperation could provide a better solution for the security of both countries.

2. Solutions are more stable.
3. It strengthens the relationship between the parties as they both become interdependent in a positive sense.
4. Positive consequences are developed for the entire system, of which they are part.

   For example, instead of unnecessary budget costs every year, the money is spent on something from which everybody benefits.

Methods for Developing Win–Win Situations

The following methods can be used to create win–win situations:

1. Making the 'cake bigger'

Some conflicts are caused by a scarcity of resources, such as not having enough time or money. Consequently, expanding resources can be one way of resolving such conflicts.

For instance, a family is unable to agree on their holiday destination—some members of the family want to go to their cottage in the mountains, while others want to have their holiday near a beach. This problem can be solved by taking longer holidays, so they can visit both destinations; for example, this could be done by reducing the number of vacation days they have during another period of the year (if they have a flexible arrangement with their employer).

2. Providing compensation that is external to the conflict

One party receives compensation for agreeing to a particular solution, but the compensation is not an integral part of the conflict. For example, a wages conflict could be resolved if the company in question agrees to employ a certain number of apprentices (unemployed). Another possibility is that compensation can be offered by a third party; for instance, in a wages dispute, the government could offer reduced taxes. This strategy depends on us having insight into the parties' priorities.

3. Priority solutions

In a situation where there are several problems that need to be solved, the parties can prioritize what is most important to them. If the wishes do not represent part of the core of the conflict, a consensus can be reached whereby each of the parties can satisfy their prioritized demands. For example, in a wages' conflict, the workers may have prioritized wage increases, while employers may have prioritized productivity. One possible solution would be to directly link wage increases to productivity increases.

4. Cost-cutting

One party gets its first priority fulfilled, while the other party gets its 'costs' regarding this solution reduced. For example, in a wages conflict, wage increases could be linked to profits. The important thing here is to highlight not only the priority interests, but also the underlying interests. Priority interests concern what is highest on the list of wishes.

Underlying interests are why this is highest on the list of wishes.

5. Building bridges

In this case, none of the parties has their wishes fulfilled, but a new possibility arises by considering the underlying interests. For example, in a lecture one of the students wants fresh air and wants to open the window. Another sitting near the window wants it kept closed because of the draft. Solution: the window(s) is/are opened in the break periods between the lectures (thus, fresh air and no draft).

Expectation of a Cause Comes Before the Cause

Prospect Theory informs us that we tend to value losses and gains differently, and are more risk-averse regarding perceived gains than in avoiding perceived losses (Tversky & Kahneman 2000). Consequently, to avoid loss, we tend to demonstrate more aggressive behaviour, while our behaviour is more defensive when it comes to making possible gains (Vis 2010). Further, research informs us that the behaviour of actors is influenced by how a problem is framed or presented. Framing a problem as a loss situation or a win–win situation will depend on the reference point we choose.

Case letter: It Is Crucial Which Reference Point We Choose

If we are considering selling a house and purchasing a new one, and we base our assessment on: 1. Comparing the property appraisals of the houses (their valuation), then our assessment will be completely different than if we, 2. compare the monthly expenses of the two houses. In other words, points 1 and 2 in the above example constitute our 'reference points', which will determine if the possible sale and purchase represents a profit or a loss, thus influencing our decision to sell/buy or not.

The reference point may be determined by the starting position, e.g. status quo, or an expected result. The status quo is one of the most common reference points from which we evaluate possible losses or gains.

Prospect Theory

An additional value is often given to something that is for sale; for instance, when people have an emotional attachment to what they are selling, such as a family holiday cabin. The sale price is often much higher than the market value of the cabin.

In another case, if our bid for some object for sale is accepted (where from our viewpoint, we considered the bid to be very low), we would still be left with the feeling of being 'tricked' in some way or the other, despite the fact that we were the one who made the low offer in the first place.

We have derived the following rules of thumb based on the Prospect Theory:

Rule 1:

If we wish to encourage aggressive behaviour, then the problem should be framed in such a way that it seems that avoiding loss is the most important outcome.

Rule 2:

If we wish to encourage defensive behaviour, then the problem should be framed in such a way that it seems that making a profit is the most important outcome.

Rule 3:

Aggressive or defensive behaviour for the same problem can be achieved by changing the reference point from which the parties will consider their decision.

The following managerial implications can be deduced from Prospect Theory:

1. Identify your reference point when making a decision based on an element of risk.
2. Find out if there are other reference points that can be used as reasonable alternatives.
3. If there are reasonable alternatives, think about your decisions based on the different reference points and see if there are any contradictions in the decisions.
4. It is only at this point that you can give the problem your full attention in relation to the various ways you have framed the problem.

Prospect theory shows us that it is important how we frame information in relation to how we make decisions in uncertain situations.

If for some reason we want to encourage aggressive or defensive behaviour, we can frame the problem in specific ways and create the desired situation.

Exercises

1. Discuss the following statements:
   a) Jeppe drinks because Holberg (the author) forced him to.
   b) When the soup you are served tastes bad, complain to the cookbook publisher.

   c) The purpose of an action is not always apparent before the action.
   d) Expectation of a cause comes before the cause.
2. Give examples from your everyday life that understanding the context is crucial to how you act.
3. Why is the following statement, 'If the Church is a context, it is because it is inside our heads', correct?
4. Give examples of how a communication situation can change from a win-lose to a win–win situation.
5. What is meant by the statement, 'when we attribute a different meaning to a situation, the situation will consequentially change for us?'
6. Give examples of when we give a situation a new name, the situation is perceived differently.
7. What does it mean when we say that 'the words we use to denote a situation set limits on the solutions we can create at a later point?'
8. Give examples from your own everyday life that the reference point you use has significance for the actions you take.
9. What is meant by the statement, 'the context is only relevant to us if we understand what it is trying to say?'
10. Using a conflict in your local community as your starting point, discuss how conflicts can be resolved using the following strategies:
    a) 'Making the cake bigger'
    b) 'Providing compensation that is external to the conflict'
    c) 'Priority solutions'
    d) 'Cost-cutting'
    e) 'Building bridges'
11. Take a familiar problem as your starting point.
    a) Frame the problem so that it promotes aggressive behaviour.
    b) Frame the problem so that it promotes defensive behaviour.

References

Bateson,G. (1972). Steps to an ecology of mind, Intex Books, London.

Arden, D. (2015). Win-win, Pearson, New York

Luhmann, N. (1996). Social systems, Stanford University Press, Stanford.

Tversky, A. & Kahneman, D. (2000). Loss aversion in riskless choice. In D. Kahneman, & A. Tversky (eds.), Choices, values and frames, Cambridge University Press, Cambridge. Pp. 143–158.

Vis, B. (2010). Politics of risk-taking, Amsterdam University, Amsterdam.

Part and Whole in a Communicative Process

6

Aims of this Chapter

1. To gain insight into communication situations regarding the fact that they should be understood by examining the relationship between the parts and the whole, and to provide an understanding that we act on the basis of our mental models in communication situations.
2. In this chapter, the reader should reflect on the following concepts:
   Systemic, positive feedback loop, negative feedback loop, negative feedback loop dominance, positive feedback loop dominance, social space, Ithaca Syndrome, binary thinking, circular relationships, linear relationships.

Systemic

By 'systemic' we mean here that the parts and the whole must be seen in relationship to each other, but where the whole always takes precedence over the parts. This is not a matter of causation, but rather a relationship in which the whole has a stronger effect on the parts than the parts have on the whole. The statement, 'The whole is more than the sum of the parts', leads one to think that by some magic formula, the difference in the quantitative sum of the parts is less than the whole. However, this is misleading, because it is not a question of comparing quantities, but rather one of the critical differences or qualitative differences. The systemic axiom is more aptly expressed as follows: **The whole is qualitatively different from the parts** (Bunge 1996, 1998, 1999). From this axiom the following statements may be deduced:

K. Ledingham et al., *Rethinking Innovation*,
https://doi.org/10.1007/978-3-031-40848-9_6

- Variation in the parts is always greater than variation in the whole.
- Stable systems are stable precisely because the subsystems are unstable.
- Creativity requires a form of chaos.
- Innovative systems have a greater degree of disorder than non-innovative systems.

Case Letter: the Tight Rope Walker

The following example can help to illustrate the axiom that the whole is qualitatively different from the parts: The tightrope walker has to constantly change the position of his/her arms and legs to remain 'stable' on the tightrope. In other words, the stability of the whole system depends on changes in the subsystems.

If You Want Stability, You Should Focus on Change

Patterns and Systemic Thinking

In systemic thinking, the main question is: What pattern binds together a given phenomenon or problem? It is precisely information, which gives us access to understanding patterns. Information that we receive or convey over time creates relationships that eventually reveal a pattern. It is the information that is structured into relationships that assign meaning to a problem area.

In order to understand a problem, we must always look at the relationships within the problem-complex, not the individual elements. This is closely linked to the question of where we set the boundaries of a problem.

Usually, we first look at the individual problems within a problem-complex, and then we look at how they are related. If we take the opposite approach, and attempt to find the relationships first, this will generate questions that lead us to qualitatively different and hopefully better results.

When the Effect Becomes the Cause

The technique for uncovering patterns is:

1. find the critical elements,
2. that are linked to each other, and
3. that over time are part of a system
4. that maintains and develops
5. the phenomenon or problem.

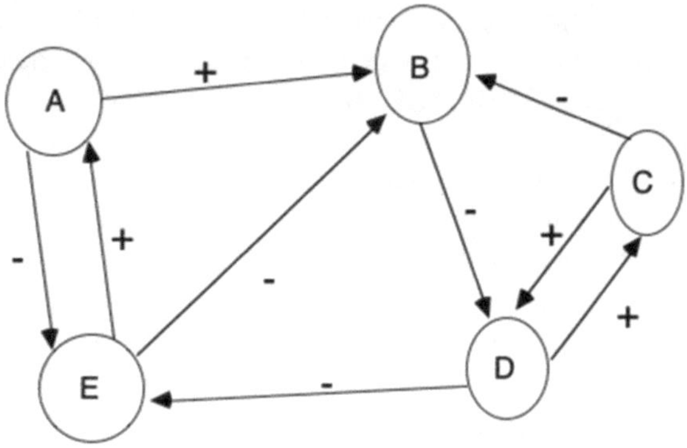

Fig. 6.1 Systemic approach

The method is to develop models of the type shown in Fig. 6.1, where a particular phenomenon / problem is in focus, and then try to discover how the elements of the phenomenon / problem are linked into a coherent pattern.

The circles in the figure above are expressions of the critical elements of a phenomenon / problem. The plus sign means that if, for example, A increases, B will also increase, and if A decreases, B will also decrease. The minus sign means that if, for example, A increases, E will decrease, and if A decreases, E will increase.

The issue of how many elements we include in a systemic model depends on where we set the boundaries for the phenomenon or problem about which we want to say something, and this is also determined by what we want to understand or explain.

A lack of insight into patterns may easily cause the problem to return later, but then in a more complex way and with greater consequences. A systemic approach is a study of the pattern that binds a phenomenon or problem together into a coherent whole, as Fig. 6.1 attempts to show.

When You Do the Opposite of What Is Expected, the Relationship Changes

We always act on the basis of models, whether we like it or not. If our models are erroneous, our actions will also be wrong (Watzlawick 2014). Even if we are in a room and decide to leave, we have a mental model that suggests there is a floor on the other side of the door, so that we do not fall into a void. Models are a form of mental economizing of resources. If our model is erroneous, and there turns out to be no floor on the other side of the door, then the consequences are obvious. This simple example is intended to show that even in everyday situations, we act on the basis of models. It is especially in social situations however that using incorrect models can lead to catastrophic consequences.

The fact that we have different models of social reality from others can be explained by three underlying mechanisms (Bandler 1993, 1993a; Bandler and Grinder 1975, 1976, 1990):

1. We generalize from reality.
2. We select something, and accordingly exclude something else.
3. We unconsciously distort things.

When we express ourselves as to the state of the social world, we base our statements on our own models of social reality. This is something rather different from claiming that this is the so-called objective social reality about which we are talking.

The same process that is active when we create our models of social reality is also active when we communicate to others how we understand a phenomenon or problem (Bandler R and J LaValle 1996).

1. We generalize against the background of our experiences.
2. Generally, we choose selectively from our memories.
3. We distort or are creative in relation to what we select from our memory, so that it is distorted in relation to what we stored in our memories at the start.

Case Letter: We are in the Business of Conceptual Constructions

The following example illustrates the link between the issue of how a problem is demarcated and systemic structuring. In Norway in the interwar years, there was a strong focus on alcohol as a social problem. To a large extent, the problem was demarcated so that the focus was on the actual consumption of alcohol. Alcohol was made very expensive, and ultimately the sale and consumption of alcohol was banned completely (the prohibition era). The results were an increase in smuggling, more criminality, corruption and a demand for larger police forces to eradicate the smuggling, corruption and criminality.

The well-known example is often considered as a flawed attempt to solve a social problem. The interesting thing, however, is that we use similar flawed reasoning all the time in other contexts, so that the solutions we produce only increase the original problem resulting in the use of more resources. The main flaw is that we create positive feedback loops, which reinforce themselves. We should always consider which feedback loop dominates an entire system. Is it the loop that dampens effects and directs the system towards a goal, i.e. a negative feedback loop dominance, or is it a feedback loop that acts as a reinforcer and causes the system to get out of control and escalate, i.e. a positive feedback loop dominance. The point of the example is that when we set the boundaries for a problem too narrowly, we create solutions that give rise to bigger problems than those we originally intended to solve, and also that the original problem remains unsolved or increases in strength.

The point we want to make is that the models we have of social reality are far from being a trivial and personal question. It is critical and applies to everyone in the social space, i.e. where our decisions have consequences.

Actions We Take in Order to Avoid Specific Results Often Produce What We Wanted to Avoid

The Ithaca Syndrome can be summarized as follows: It is the process that is important, not the result. Reaching Ithaca was the goal of Odysseus's journey. During the whole of his journey, he was driven by his longing for the island of Ithaca, and the people who lived there. But the whole of Homer's epic poem rests on what Odysseus experienced during his journey. And this epic poem is the source of what we call the Ithaca Syndrome: the idea that it is the process that matters, not the goal.

Ithaca gives meaning to the journey, but in real life the opposite is generally the case. The journey may be important enough, it may be interesting and provide inspiration, but the point of every journey is to arrive, otherwise it would not be a journey, but perhaps some form of lifelong recreation.

Statement: The idea that it is the process that matters and not necessarily the result is an example of our tendency towards binary thinking: one thing OR the other. Further, the Ithaca Syndrome can be seen as an example of absolving ourselves of responsibility for the results that will be attained.

Neither the process nor the result are what matters, but the fact that the process influences the results, and the result will also—first as expectation and later as reality—influence the process. This pattern is circular, as Fig. 6.2 attempts to demonstrate.

In circular patterns, it is pointless to ask what came first and what is most important. In the mental world, the expectation of the outcome may very well have an impact on the process. When a result is achieved and the activities continue over time, the actual result will also affect the process.

Further, it is at times disconcertingly clear that it is precisely those individuals who do not achieve results who are the foremost advocates of the Ithaca Syndrome—'at least I learned a lot during the process!' is something we often hear. However, learning is always oriented to internal or external change. If something has been learned from the process, this will be visible later from the results.

Fig. 6.2 Process and result

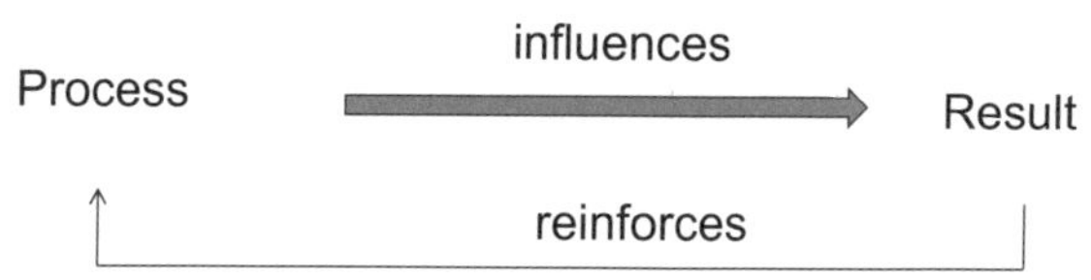

Otherwise, learning has not taken place. In the Ithaca Syndrome, we can end up solving non-existent problems, and overlooking the actual problems. However, this not only concerns the Ithaca Syndrome, but also applies to many types of binary thinking, where we do not look for the pattern of relationships in which problems and phenomena are included.

If we try to find solutions to problems in the problem-structuring phase, before we have uncovered the pattern of relationships within which the problems are enmeshed, we may end up in a situation where the solution becomes the real problem.

We tend to overlook and/or underestimate circular relationships, where, for example, A affects B and B affects A.

Linear relationships tend to dominate our thinking, because they are simple and easy to understand.

Looking Towards the Future with Optimism Because It Is an Echo from the Past

A question that often arises is the following:

Should we start with the easy or difficult problems first?

The answer is that neither the strategy is effective, for the simple reason that once a problem is solved it cannot be used as a 'negotiating card' at a later date. The counter-argument to this is that it is easier to create a win–win situation if we start with a simple problem. This is because it will be easier to create a positive climate, if we are able to agree on something. However, the most effective strategy is to structure the entire communication situation so that alternative problems can be discussed simultaneously (Dowell et al. 2018).

An important question is whether there are links between the ongoing communication situation and communication situations conducted previously by the same people. If such links are not considered, unnecessary conflicts may be generated in an otherwise visibly good solution.

If we want a stable situation for the whole system, then we must ensure that an open communication climate exists.

If we want to understand the pattern that is established in a communication situation, then we can develop loop models that show positive and negative feedback loops.

If we want insight into how others think, then we can try to find out which models they use.

We have shown two examples of such models below.

Exercises

1. Discuss the following:
   a) If you want stability, you should focus on change.
   b) What happens when an effect becomes a cause?
   c) If you do the opposite of what is expected, the reaction is changed.
   d) Actions we take in order to avoid specific results often produce what we wanted to avoid.
   e) Looking towards the future with optimism because it is an echo from the past.
2. Using a communication conflict you have been involved in, or a problem or phenomenon that you are familiar with, provide answers for a)–d).
   a) Find the critical elements that existed (exist) as you see them.
   b) How are these elements interrelated? Use arrows with plus and minus signs to indicate how the elements interact.
   c) Develop a model that says something about the relationship between the elements you selected.
   d) Discuss the model.
3. Find examples from your everyday life of people or situations that fit the Ithaca Syndrome.
4. Give examples from your everyday life where the process affects the result, but where the result also affects the process.
5. Give examples of binary thinking.
6. Give examples of circular patterns in a communication situation that you have participated in, where element A affects B, and B affects A.
7. Give examples of the following when you formulate a social problem or phenomenon:
   a) When you generalize from reality.
   b) When you choose something from social reality and do not choose something else.
   c) When you distort or modify what you have selected from social reality.
8. Give examples of the same phenomenon (7 a–c) when you select something from memory to convey something to another person.

References

Bandler, R. (1993). Time for a change, Meta Publications Inc., New York.
Bandler, R. (1993a). The adventures of anybody, Meta Publications Inc., New York.
Bandler, R. & LaValle, J. (1996). Persuasion engineering, Meta Publications, New York.
Bunge, M. (1996). Finding philosophy in social science, New Haven CT: Yale University Press
Bunge, M. (1998). Social science under debate, University of Toronto Press, Toronto.
Bunge, M. (1999). The sociology-philosophy connection, Transaction Publishers, New Brunswick, NJ.

Bandler, R. & Grinder, J. (1975). The structure and magic, Science and Behaviour Books, New York.

Bandler, R. & Grinder, J. (1976). The structure and magic II, Science and Behaviour Books, New York.

Bandler, R. & Grinder, J. (1990). Frogs into Princes Eden Grove Editions, Middlesex

Dowell, N.M.M., Nixon, T.M. & Graesser, A.C. (2018). Group communication analysis. Behaviour Research Methods, 51, 3: 1007–1041.

Watzlawick, P. (2014). Pragmatics of human communication, W.W. Norton, New York.

'Aspect Seeing'

7

Aims of this Chapter

1. To provide an understanding that social facts are mentally constructed and do not exist as an objective reality.
2. In this chapter, the reader should reflect on the following concepts:
   Social facts, concrete fallacy, constructs, overestimation error.

Objective Reality Is Always Subjectively Interpreted

Perspective insight is the ability to see the other party's view in a communication or negotiation situation (Pruit and Rubin 1986). Research shows that in a communication process, those who have greater insight into the perspective of the other party, will achieve more success and award more concessions, and be able to express a better understanding of the other party's values and expectations, than those with a low degree of perspective insight (Putnam 1985). Furthermore, a proposal in a communication process is considered to be more objective (here understood as serving both parties) if it is made by 'our side', although the proposal may be identical to the one proposed by the other party (Putnam 1985).

The purpose of the 'perspective meeting' is to agree on what the social facts are. The 'concrete' facts that appear to us are not as concrete as they may seem right away. To claim that the facts as they appear to our consciousness are concrete is to succumb to the concrete fallacy. A rhetorical stratagem related to the concrete fallacy, which is often used in communication contexts, is to take as a starting point a presumed conclusion, which one has managed to convince others represents a real situation, and then argue for the necessity of certain measures to reach this conclusion.

K. Ledingham et al., *Rethinking Innovation*,
https://doi.org/10.1007/978-3-031-40848-9_7

This rhetorical stratagem can only be counteracted by not taking the conclusion as a given fact, but opposing it, or better, by requiring that the other party reveal the actual existence of the 'conclusion'. Another method similar to the concrete fallacy is to interpret metaphors literally, that is, interpret a metaphor as if it is something 'real'. The examples in organizational literature are several, e.g. 'organizations as machines' (Lakoff and Johnson 2003). The metaphorical fallacy would then be to consider humans as replaceable machine parts. Similarly, organizations are sometimes realistically compared to computers—then it is just a matter of creating the right software (programs), i.e. rules and routines, then the whole system will function smoothly.

Despite actors having different perspectives, a 'perspective meeting', or even better, a convergence of perspectives, is possible. One approach is to uncover the motives of the actors. The motives can then be divided into two main categories. One category is the objectives the actors wish to achieve. This is linked to the future, goals and results, which is a subjective category linked to the actor's consciousness. The second category is linked to the actor's background, mental disposition and the environment that has shaped the actor. This is oriented towards the past and is a so-called objective category where given elements can be examined.

All our knowledge consists of constructs, i.e. a set of abstractions, generalizations and formalizations. The point being made here is that there are no simple facts in 'reality'. All 'facts' are created through our own interpretive process, i.e. inside our heads, and do not exist externally to us in the social sphere. This means that social facts are always our interpretations of the social reality as it appears to us.

Although this distinction may be trivial, it is crucial to be aware of it in a communication context if we are to achieve a 'perspective meeting'. The facts are subjectively selected from the social sphere, and then linked to experiences that we subjectively choose from our memory. It is precisely that which we think is relevant to us in the situation that we choose from the surroundings and from memory. However, this subjective understanding of the facts enables both parties in a communication situation to learn to change perspectives in order to facilitate a 'perspective meeting', or better still, a 'convergence of perspectives'.

One technique for facilitating a 'perspective meeting' is to let the parties attempt to place themselves in an imaginary future setting, and envision that the conflict or disagreement in question has been resolved, and then look at how they (in their imaginations) managed to resolve the conflict. This technique is called 'Future Perfect Thinking' and was developed by Karl E. Weick (1979).

In social relationships it is the unknown factors that play a prominent role, while in models of a social situation one operates with the known factors. Open communication between parties can reduce this tendency of simplification that seems to be prominent. Through communication, a 'perspective meeting' can be established, and the simplifications of the models can be used for what they are really meant to be, a map of a physical terrain.

What We Know Depends on Whom We Got to Know It from

One phenomenon that seems to be common is that we tend to have too much confidence in the correctness of our own assessments. This means that we tend to structure a problem in a way that is not as effective as it could have been.

If we overestimate the correctness of our own perspective, our willingness to compromise will be reduced. To increase our ability to compromise, we need to learn how to see the other person's perspective. One strategy for learning how to change perspective is to focus on the question: Why do you think your decision may be wrong?

An illusory superiority of our own perspective is more likely to occur when we have little knowledge of the phenomenon in question.

Overestimating the correctness of our own view can also be explained by the point of departure we have in a communication situation, and that we do not understand the other party's perspective. Furthermore, overestimating the superiority of our own view may stem from an unrealistic positive self-image, an over-optimistic attitude towards the future and a belief that we have control over the outcome.

In a communication context, it is crucial to understand that all the so-called social facts are only partial truths. Thus although expressing one's own view is important, listening is also crucial to effective communication.

Exercises

1. Explain the following statements:
   a) Objective reality is always subjectively interpreted.
   b) What we know depends on whom we got to know it from.
2. Find five metaphors for communication.
3. (Constructing a metaphor about something can be done by comparing it to something else by using the word '*is*'. For instance, '*Communication is a bridge between people*'.
4. As your starting point, take two everyday decisions you have made during the past year. Discuss these decisions based on the following question: Why do you think your decisions may have been wrong?
5. Starting with a motive you may have for acting the way you do in a particular situation:
   a) What purpose did you seek to achieve?
   b) Which aspects of your past and your surroundings influenced this particular motive?
6. As your starting point, take an ongoing conflict or disagreement that you are currently concerned about:
   a) Imagine a future situation where this conflict or disagreement is resolved.
   b) In your imagination, how did you manage to resolve the conflict?

References

Lakoff, G. & Johnson, M. (2003). Metaphors we live by, University of Chicago Press, Chicago.

Pruitt, D.G. & Rubin, J.Z. (1986).. Social conflict: Escalation, stalemate and settlement, McGraw Hill, New York.

Putnam, L.L. (1985). Bargaining as organizational communication. In R.D. McPhee & P.K. Tomkins (ed.), Organizational communication: Traditional themes and new directions. Vol. 13, Sage, New York.

Weick, K.E. (1979). The social psychology of organizing, McGraw-Hill, New York.

8 Information Processes as Part of Communication

Aims of this Chapter

1. To gain insight about the information processes operating in a communication process.
2. In this chapter, the reader should reflect on the following concepts: Message, communication error, data, code, information, metaphor.

The Smaller the Unit of Measurement Used to Measure a Coastline, the Longer the Coastline Becomes

Information, knowledge and communication are linked in a system where each of the elements has a specific relationship to the other elements. The relationship may be expressed as follows: Information is an expression of the communicable part of knowledge.

The relationship between communication and information can be expressed by saying that the smallest part of a communication unit is a message (Bateson 1972: 130–134). A message may be understood as consisting of three components. First, is the information component, which is what one wants to convey to the other party. Second, the message consists of a relational component, which says something about the relationship we have with the person(s) we are communicating with. Third, the message also consists of a hierarchical component, which says something about the social status of the parties in the communication situation. In order to fully interpret a message, it is therefore important that we are aware of all three components.

When a message is interpreted and it has been made clear that the interpreter has understood the message, two things may occur:

K. Ledingham et al., *Rethinking Innovation*,
https://doi.org/10.1007/978-3-031-40848-9_8

1. The first party (the sender) may dispute the validity of the interpretation, or
2. He/she can accept the interpretation.

A rhetorical stratagem that the sender may use in certain contexts, in order to gain control of a communication situation, is to dispute the validity of the receiver's interpretation by saying 'that's not what I said', or, 'that's not what I meant' and so on. This denial of the validity of the interpretation confuses the other party and makes him/her feel insecure. In other words, a difference in interpretation arises, over which the sender has complete control, because it was he/she who conveyed the message. In this way, the sender can take advantage of the situation; however, this may hinder a genuine communication process.

When a person utters a message and we interpret it, much of the information we receive will depend on the relationship we have with the person who uttered the message. Another way of saying this is that there exists a hierarchical structure in all communication processes, which may be related to trust, the type of relationship the parties have to each other, their history, values and so on. This can explain why the same message may be interpreted in different ways by different people.

In a communication situation, we do not have the choice between communicating and *not communicating*. Silence, for example, can function as crucial information to the other party. For instance, remaining silent under a police interrogation would not necessarily be interpreted in such a way that it did not provide any useful information. Information and communication can therefore only be understood in relation to the pattern in which they appear.

In the world of physics, there is no effect without energy. However, this does not apply to information and communication. Not submitting your tax return can have major consequences, or the gift you did not send to your parents on their golden wedding anniversary can send a negative message. In other words, *no message* can function as information in a communication situation.

In an ongoing communication situation between two parties, it is not only difficult to point out what is the cause and effect of a particular part of the process, but it is also meaningless. However, this is often done by one or more of the parties in a communication situation, with the aim of putting themselves in a better light. For example, 'I said it because you said …' and so on. One party breaks up the communication process in such a way that puts his/her own statements in a better light. But this is to compare an information and communication process with a physical process, where object A causes object B to move. This is what we can term a classic communication error, which often ends up in major conflicts, on personal or global levels, such as marital quarrels or the arms race.

The Interpretation Is Different from What Is Interpreted

The loop model in Fig. 8.1 shows how messages function in a communication process (the loop model is non-linear).

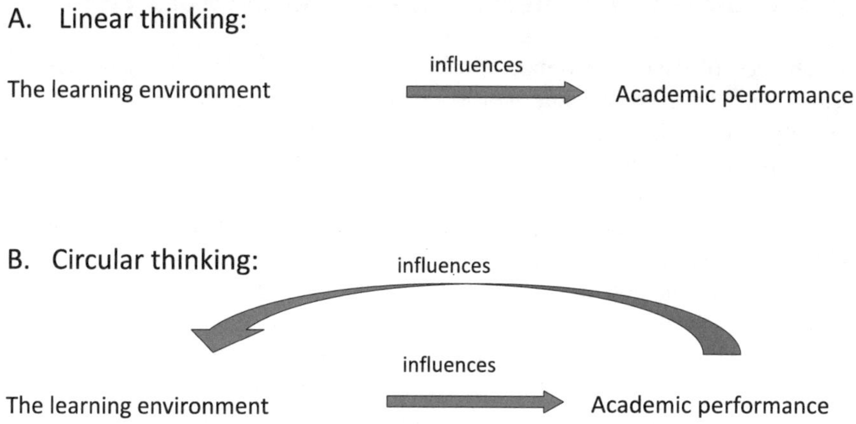

Fig. 8.1 A loop model of how messages function in a communication process

If we choose to say that a side effect is the cause of a problem, then we make a classic communication error. We probably have a picture of a straight line in our consciousness, where cause and effect are operating. We often make such communicative errors, consciously or unconsciously. Unconsciously, because we do not know any better, consciously, because we wish to manipulate the outcome of a dialogue. We need to constantly devote many resources to correcting the mistake of considering information and communication as if they were physical objects that we can change any way we want to. On the personal marital level, it seems the only ones that profit from such communicative errors are the gift shops and florists. Of course, there are much worse consequences when we are operating at a more complex system level.

Communication using body language is not qualitatively different from verbal communication. That said, it should be emphasized that we may react more strongly emotionally to negative body language than to verbal language. The explanation may be that body language evolved before verbal language in communicative development, and is thus more rooted in our basic mental structure (de-Graft Aikins 2011: 67–87).

First, an important point concerning information and communication situations is that they always occur within the social system. By this, we mean that a communication process must always be considered based on the situation in which it expresses itself. Second, the previous experiences of each party are constantly part of the communication process, even though this is not explicitly expressed as information. Third, the process is also guided by the future prospects, or expectations, that both parties have. In this way, the communication process occurs continuously in the present, past and future, even though the information part occurs only in the present. To disregard this is to lose sight of the fact that a communication process cannot be directly compared to relationships in the physical world.

What Is the Similarity Between a Fish and the Word 'Fish'?

An absence of data or information can be informative, whereas a large amount of data may have no meaning. For example, the fact that the Norwegian Police Security Service is unable to find background information (data) about a particular person can be very informative regarding that person. The large digit 1,018,111,214,191 provides us with no information whatsoever, unless we know what context it is used in. If the large digit represents some kind of code, it is still without meaning unless we have the key to the code. 'Information' ceases to be information the moment no one understands the information in a message. At that point, the information is no more than incomprehensible fragments or utterances.

Data, which is linked to a code, which some people understand, becomes information for them, but is incomprehensible to those who do not understand the code. For instance, viewing a swallow does not provide you with information concerning its aerodynamic features. Nevertheless, the swallow 'contains' information about aerodynamic principles, which may be accessible to those who possess a 'code', that is, knowledgeable scientists who study the aerodynamic features of swallows.

In many contexts, it is precisely the code or understanding of the code that provides the answer to whether we understand a certain type of information and at what level we understand it.

However, the problem with codes is, among other things, linked to two essential questions in the context of information:

1. What information of vital importance is not expressed in the message? The answer to the question tells us a little about the 'code' used between the parties.
2. What information is conveyed through a particular type of metaphor? The answer to the question gives us insight into what 'code' the person using the metaphor uses, and thus an insight into how he/she 'thinks'.

American Presidents: Lingo, Bingo, Dingo

Any step towards more information can be thought of as moving the observer away from holistic and meaningful information, into the area of analytical information or incomprehensible utterances. Another way of saying this is that the more we learn about what we see, the less we see. In order to illustrate this apparent paradox, we have developed Fig. 8.2.

The point of Fig. 8.2 is to show that information is qualitatively different from, e.g. a hamburger that one can divide endlessly to analyse the smallest parts. Another point, which is not so clear in the figure, is that number is different from quantity and quantity is different from quality. For instance, three pails of milk is different from three litres of milk, and three litres of milk is different from good or bad milk. However, we cannot assume that quantity turns into quality, as such an idea is no more than a category error. Whether it is three litres of milk, thirty

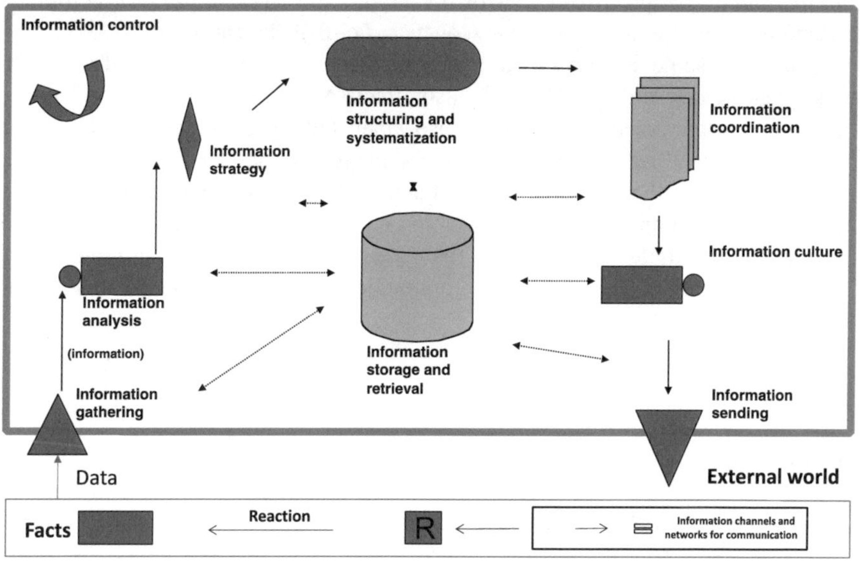

Fig. 8.2 Critical information structure (info-structure) processes

litres of milk or three hundred litres of milk, this will never have any importance regarding the quality of the milk, that is, whether the milk is good or bad.

Another point regarding Fig. 8.2 is that we do not necessarily understand more of an utterance, even though we are familiar with all the info-structure processes in the communication situation in which we participate.

Information does not belong to the physical universe in the same way as material elements, and to confuse information with material elements is on the same level as claiming quantity can be equated with quality.

It is not the case that the more information and communication that takes place, the better it is for the parties involved. Beyond a certain point, openness regarding information and communication can become detrimental to relationships.

Exercises

1. Discuss the following statements:
   a) The smaller the unit of measurement used to measure a coastline, the longer the coastline becomes.
   b) The interpretation is different from what is interpreted.
   c) What is the similarity between a fish and the word 'fish'?
   d) One should believe in both faith and knowledge.
2. Give six examples that silence (not saying anything) or not responding can be very informative to the other party.

3. Give three examples from your own everyday life where a piece of communication is structured into a linear sequence, i.e. B is the cause of A.
4. Using the same examples you gave in question 3, try to identify circular sequences, i.e. A affects B, but B also affects A.
5. Which metaphors do you mainly use when talking about organizations and companies? What do these metaphors express about an organization or a company? Are there other metaphors that may be more appropriate?
6. Give three examples that nothing (doing nothing) can function as a cause.
7. Find four examples that illustrate the statement: Beyond a certain point, openness regarding information and communication can become detrimental to relationships.

References

Aikins, de-Graft, A. (2011). Nonverbal communication in everyday multicultural life. In D. Hook, B. Franks & M.W. Bauer (eds.) The social psychology of communication, Palgrave, London. pp. 67–87.

Bateson, G. (1972). Steps to an ecology of mind, Intex Books, London.

9 Information Processes

Aims of this Chapter

1. To gain knowledge about the way information is stored in memory.
2. In this chapter, the reader should reflect on the following concepts:

Visual short-term memory, conceptual short-term memory, long-term memory, working memory, information distortion, recursivity, holographic, empirical information, value-oriented information, strategic / tactical information, group-thinking, information overload.

What We Seek to Achieve Is Different from Why We Seek to Achieve It

It is important to understand how the human memory functions, when we are carrying out information processes, because information-searching is closely related to the knowledge we have in our memory.

We have a short-term visual information memory that holds information for only a few milliseconds. We also have a short-term conceptual memory. This holds information for approximately one second. Another type of short-term memory that is more general, but also has limited capacity, can only operate with approximately 5 to 9 terms at a time (Miller 1978). This short-term memory only holds the information for approximately 20 seconds. The classic example is new phone numbers—which we only manage to remember for approximately 20 seconds.

The short-term memory acts as a buffer, which either erases information or passes it on to the long-term memory. When gathering information or transferring information, we should be aware of the limited capacity of our short-term memory.

However, if something captures our interest, then we will be able to remember the information better than if the information fails to capture our interest.

K. Ledingham et al., *Rethinking Innovation*,
https://doi.org/10.1007/978-3-031-40848-9_9

The memory can be divided into the following sequences: Information enters the sensory-motor system (sight, hearing, touch). It then goes on to the short-term memory and the working memory, and then it is possibly stored in the long-term memory. The working memory holds information temporarily, and is also able to access stored information (Anderson 1990).

The long-term memory can also be divided into two elements. One element is associated with personal episodes or events in one's life, while another element, the semantic component, stores knowledge about meaningful relationships in our world. There is a difference in memory capacity in terms of remembering and communicating to others about a fishing trip, than being able to categorize the various types of fish one caught regarding species and type. In other words, we remember better episodes from our own life than semantic information. This insight may also be used to advantage when we gather and disseminate information (Abelson 1981).

It is important to be aware of the fact that our memory has limited capacity and that we tend to distort the information we already have in our memory.

The memory system has three main functions (Arkes and Blumer 1985):

1. To take in the necessary information,
2. To store it and
3. To retrieve information from memory.

Each of these functions has a tendency to distort information, especially if we work with large amounts of information at a time. In particular, it seems that we tend to distort information when we extract it from the long-term memory (Slovic and Lichtenstein 1971).

It is not necessarily the case that the more information we store, the more effective we become. It is possible that the more information we store, the less creative we become, because being creative relies on a random component (Csikszentmihalyi 2013). It may be possible, at least in an organizational context, that the more information we store and remember, the less room there is for random components and thus creativity and innovation.

Storing and remembering information should not be confused with searching for information. If, in the search process, we have a question or problem we are working on, then we do not need to store or remember this information for a long period. However, what we need to do is link the information we already have with the information we find relevant in the search process. It is this link that leads to the 'creative new'. It is namely new relationships between elements that are the essence of creativity.

Storing the information we receive in the memory should not be compared to an archive or units stored in any type of database. Instead, it is more appropriate to refer to the human memory in terms of knowledge structures and cognitive schemata (Miller 1978).

Case Letter: Information and Memory

Metaphorically, we can compare memory to a fishing net in which each knot is linked to every other knot in the net by means of twine, which forms the channel for transmission. Using this metaphor, a unit of information in one corner of the net can be linked to a unit of information in another corner of the net in order to create a qualitatively new unit of information. Further, we can imagine several nets piled pancake-fashion on top of each other, such that the further down we go into the pile of nets, the greater the depth of knowledge we find about a topic that lies at the top of the pile, for example. In this way, we can imagine how information is organized as networks of units of information that exist simultaneously at the same logical level and also hierarchically. This gives us an image of a storage capacity that is organized in a way that is simultaneously hierarchic, recursive and holographic. In this context, we use the word 'holographic' to convey that the individual elements are found again within the whole. We use the word 'recursive' to mean that each individual fishing net in the pile of nets has connections to all the other nets, while at the same time it is fully connected within itself. Understood in this manner, a memory becomes creative. It can create something completely different from the individual units of information that are entered into the pile of nets. This is the qualitative difference between human memory and the storage capacity of a computer, for example.

Cognitive *schemata* can be seen as cognitive structures that contain information about special situations, or a class of situations. Cognitive schemata should be able to function such that we notice and remember things that support what we already know. The knowledge structures or schemata that make up our pre-knowledge (Johannessen 2020) can either be considered as passive, that is, we extract information from a 'knot in the net', or as active, that is, we connect several 'knots in the net' so as to create a new information unit. No matter how we apply the knowledge structures, they will have a direct impact on both how we gather information from the environment and how we use it.

We give priority to what we already know, and thus we economize both our information search processes and information analysis, although this may in many cases lead to systematic errors, which we will examine later. However, these errors need not only be negative. It may well be the case that it is precisely the random components of our systematic errors that lead to the 'creative new' and innovations.

Considered in this way, it is precisely the fact that our memory does not function like a storage device of a computer that enables us to create new knowledge. If we could completely rely on our memories (as if they were like the storage device of a computer), then we might not have been able to create 'the new'. It is precisely this innovative ability that has enabled man to progress from the Stone Age to the modern technological society of today.

Thoughts Are Different from What We Are Thinking About

We are continually presented with more information that we are expected to relate to. The information we receive, or gather, may be roughly divided into three types:

1. Empirical or factual information,
2. Value-oriented information and
3. Tactical/strategic information.

The three types do not necessarily exclude each other, i.e. empirical information may well be both value-oriented and strategic, but it does not have to be. What we must constantly ask ourselves in relation to the information we are presented with is the following: How relevant is this information in relation to the problems or issues we are working on or which we are interested in?

Further, information is not objective in the sense it has to be interpreted in order for it to be meaningful. Although several people are given exactly the same piece of information, they will most probably interpret it differently.

The media presents us with their interpreted version of the information they have received from various agencies that have also interpreted information they have gathered or received (in other words, the information passes through several agencies). This information that we are presented with in the media is then interpreted by us on the basis of our prior knowledge and values. In a media context, the expression 'pictures don't lie' is in itself a lie, for the simple reason that the media selects and edits images with the aim of presenting their particular version of social reality.

Information gathering can be said to be based on two main elements:

1. Background knowledge of the subject and
2. The purpose of the acquisition of the information.

Our search for information is characterized by the fact that we tend to search for information that supports our established beliefs, rather than search for information that conflicts with our beliefs (Bazerman et al. 1984).

One way of guarding against the current information explosion and the media-created reality, at least in work related to specific projects, is to form information groups that critically evaluate the relevance of the information gathered for a project (Janis 1982). These groups should, as far as possible, be composed of people with different backgrounds, experience and knowledge, so that each member's knowledge compliments the knowledge of the others in the group. These complementary groups will make it possible to evaluate information more critically, so that group-thinking can be avoided. Group-thinking can lead to the following consequences (Janis 1982):

- An illusion of invulnerability
- An uncritical attitude regarding the group's ethics, so that the ethical consequences of decisions are often overlooked
- Vital information is often overlooked that may lead to major negative consequences in the long run
- A stereotypical view of people other than the group's members
- Suppression of doubts and counter-arguments
- A development of similar and rigid points of view
- Pressure exerted on those members who express strong arguments against the group's norms
- The emergence of certain individuals who guard against information that goes against the group's views by filtering out such information.

In order to counter the tendency of group-thinking that may also develop in the complementary groups, these groups should replace members after a certain time has elapsed, so that the group composition is always based on the complementary principle.

Another way to safeguard that one gathers relevant information is to categorize the information by considering the following questions:

1. What is the *meaning* of the information we are collecting?
2. What *types* of information are we collecting?
3. How *much* information do we need to collect?
4. What specific *changes* in the environment have taken place in relation to the information we have collected?
5. How *quickly* can we manage to collect the information?
6. How great is the *time-lag* between when an event occurs until we get information about it?
7. What is the *extent* (percentage) of errors detected in the information collected?
8. What are the *costs* of collecting the information?
9. How *much* of the information collected will be used in decision-making?
10. How much *time* does it take between when we collect information until it is used in decision-making?
11. What *types* of information collected are most frequently used in decision-making?

The answers to the questions can help to analyse the way we collect information and be used as a basis for developing and possibly changing an information system for groups or organizations.

Studies of the future access to information in organizations and in society at large suggest that the amount of information will only increase in the years to come. This 'information-overload' can, according to Miller (1978: 89–121), result in the following consequences:

a. We will be unable to differentiate between relevant and irrelevant information.
b. Due to the large amount of information, we will make errors more often when assessing information.
c. Queues of information will emerge, which will not be processed quickly enough.
d. We will filter out information that should not have been filtered out.
e. We will overload the media we use disseminating the information.
f. We will develop a tendency to generalize so that necessary details disappear.

Each of these factors will incur a cost by diminishing efficiency in relation to the activities that the information is intended to effectively facilitate. The consequence of this danger of information-overload is that we need to develop our ability to find relevant information by being able to interpret it appropriately, evaluate its usefulness and apply the relevant information to the problems that we are focusing on.

Writing to Find Out What One Is Thinking

One often enters into a communication situation with only one single strategy. An alternative approach that has proved to be more effective is to assume that the strategy used is not necessarily correct. Therefore, one is constantly searching for information that opposes the strategy one has chosen. This will make it easier to change strategy along the way, if it becomes apparent that it does not produce the desired results.

A substantial part of a communication process is oriented around information exchange. However, we tend to overestimate information that supports our attitudes and assumptions, and underestimate information that opposes them (Cialdini 1993). We rarely actively search for information that goes against our existing beliefs and attitudes.

Differences in available information for the various parties can create an information gap that may lead to increased conflicts at a later date. Increased exchange of information has proved to be effective in achieving a win–win situation, which is shown in Thompson (1991, 1991a) and Zubek et al. (1992). How can we obtain such information in order to achieve a win–win situation? Bazerman (1994) has developed five strategies:

1. Build trust and share information with others.
2. Ask questions, listen rather than attempt to persuade.
3. Give away 'need to know' information and you will get back information that you find useful.
4. Present multiple themes at once. Then you will get to know a little about how others think, when some of the themes are rejected.
5. Get a third party to mediate, so that both parties have the opportunity to go back to their original negotiating point that they had before the third party put forward his/her proposal.

Concrete thinking relies on holistic processes

We may use information in such a way that it does not lead to information-overload with the resulting detrimental consequences for the communication process.

We can develop structured ways of collecting information.

We can develop effective communication strategies.

If we want to create confusion we can:

1. Provide new information that contains more than 5–9 items, depending on the recipient's capacity.
2. Provide new information and before 20 seconds have elapsed, add more information. The initial information will then be lost from memory for most people.

If we want to convey something and at the same time appear credible, we should do the opposite of what is proposed in points 1 and 2.

Exercises

1. Discuss the following statements:
   a) What we seek to achieve is different from why we seek to achieve it.
   b) Thoughts are different from what we are thinking about.
   c) Writing to find out what one is thinking.
2. You are asked to provide information to the board of the company you work for. How would you convey this information if the aim is:
   a) That they will remember the information for a long time.
   b) That they should quickly forget it.
3. Mention three examples where you distorted information that you had taken from your memory and where others made you aware of the fact that you had distorted the information. Did it create a conflict when you were made aware of the fact that you had distorted the information? How did the subsequent communication evolve?
4. Think of two units of information you have received during the course of the day. Connect these two units of information and try to create completely new information that did not exist in the individual information units.
5. What do you think is meant by the phrase 'giving priority to what we already know'?
6. What does it mean when we say that our interpretation of information is dependent on our prior knowledge and our values?
7. Give examples of information-overload from your everyday life. Review the six consequences that information-overload can lead to and discuss the examples in relation to all the six points.
8. Based on a strategy that is used at your workplace, find information that goes against this strategy.

9. Take a view or attitude that you hold strongly. Search for information that is opposed to this view or attitude. Discuss.

References

Abelson, R.P. (1981). The psychological status of the script concept. American Psychologist, 36: 715–721.

Anderson, J.R. (1990). Cognitive psychology and its implications, Freeman, New York.

Arkes, H.R. & Blumer, C. (1985). The Psychology of sunk costs. Organizational Behaviour and Human Performance, 35: 129–140.

Bazerman, M.H., Giuliano, T. & Appleman, A. (1984). Escalation in individual and group decision making. Organizational Behaviour and Human Performance, 33: 141–152.

Bazerman, M.H. (1994). Judgement in managerial decision making, Wiley, New York.

Cialdini, R.B. (1993). Influence: Science and practice, HarperCollins, New York.

Csikszentmihalyi, M. (2013). Creativity: The psychology of discovery and invention, Harper, New York.

Janis, I.L. (1982). Group think, Houghton Muffins, New York.

Johannessen, J-A. (2020). The workplace of the future, Routledge, London.

Miller, J.G. (1978). Living systems, McGraw-Hill, New York.

Slovic, P. & Lichtenstein, S. (1971). Comparison of Bayesian and regression approaches in the study of information processing in judgement. Organizational Behaviour and Human Performance, 6: 649–744.

Thompson, L.L. (1990). An examination of naive and experienced negotiators. Journal of Personality and Social Psychology, 59: 82–90.

Thompson, L.L. (1991a). Information exchange in negotiation. Journal of experimental Social Psychology, 27: 161–179.

Zubek, J.M., Pruitt, D.G., Peirce, R.S., McGillicaddy, N.B. & Syna, H. (1992). Short term success in mediation: Its relationship to disputant and mediator behaviours and prior conditions. Journal of Conflict Resolution, 36: 546–572.

Communication Strategies 10

Aims in this Chapter

1. To learn how to develop a vision that can be communicated.
   To gain insight into the importance of game theory for communication strategies.
2. In this chapter, the reader should reflect on the following concepts:
   The trimming effect, vision, 'steady course' paradox, bottom line, prisoner's dilemma, social dilemma, CI strategy, CCI strategy, echo effect.

It's What You Are Best at That Will Be Your Downfall

Plans can have different functions. They can have a symbolic effect, that is, we can show that we have plans for various projects, although we have not implemented them yet. They may have a marketing function, i.e. in order to attract attention. They can have a testing function, i.e. using a plan to investigate any possible resistance to the plan, if we were to implement it. The test may also be aimed at acquiring funding. Plans may also be used if we need to intervene in vulnerable areas. As a general rule, plans are linked to a strategy to achieve one or more goals.

Plans that conflict with the goals of the system are not necessarily the result of poor coordination on the part of management. It may be a deliberate strategy to create ambiguity in the system in order to motivate the actors to become more involved. Such involvement will consequently trim the whole system, and draw attention (Weick 1979; Watzlawick 2014).

The alternative is to spend a lot of energy on interpreting past events and putting them together so they match the current goals, strategies and plans. This may promote consistency, but will possibly inhibit the 'trimming effect'.

K. Ledingham et al., *Rethinking Innovation*,
https://doi.org/10.1007/978-3-031-40848-9_10

The trimming effect is aimed at both increased awareness and increased interdependence between people in the system. The increased interdependence could in turn be an important mechanism for building crucial alliances in the system, which can later become an important driver for achieving set goals. Further, the management of the system will obtain an overview of which people belong to which alliances. When management has obtained this information, they will have a better opportunity to control the main types of relationships that exist in the system.

The point is that one can make many decisions without solving a single problem, if you do not have an overview of the alliances and relationships that exist in the system.

Further, the trimming effect has the function of creating expectations in the system, and it is precisely expectations that can have a crucial effect on the final result. In the same way that methods influence results, and preconceptions affect what one sees, then relationships in the system influence what is reported. However, the trimming effect is not consciously applied to any great extent in systems. The explanation may be that most people do not want or cannot manage to live with the uncertainty and lack of visible order that the trimming effect brings about (Luhmann 1996; Strugar-Jelača 2018). Therefore, consistent plans are used in many contexts that are not linked to the activities taking place in the system, but which are consistent with goals and strategy as well as previous plans.

The Boundary of Culture Is Consistent with the Boundary of Communication

Figure 10.1 can be used to help clarify the goals, strategy and plan in relation to a vision for negotiations.

Explanation of the model:
A vision can be anything from an ambiguous dream to a clear and concrete goal. A vision is meant to create a focus. It is oriented towards a concrete result. Further, it has both an intention and aims at an end-product. An important purpose is to create intensity and to focus on the future. A vision tries to capture attention, by targeting behaviour. To be able to create a vision, it is a necessary condition (but not a sufficient one) to know what you want to do.

Knowing why you want to achieve something and at the same time what you are trying to achieve gives energy to the vision. If you know what you want, why you want it and what you are trying to achieve, while knowing how to achieve it, then you have given the vision a strategic dimension.

The purpose of the vision and its strategic positioning is to create 'the new'; that which only exists because we have created it. In short, this is the distinction between adapting to the external environment, and creating one's own or the system's future.

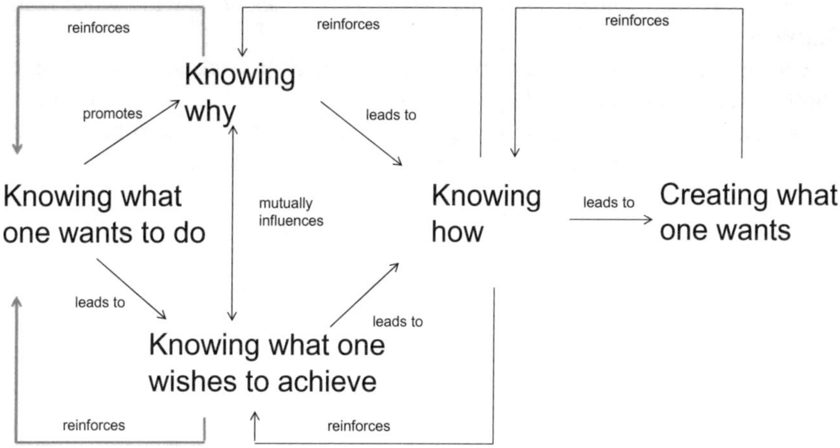

Fig. 10.1 How, why and what we aim to achieve in a communication process

A vision is meant to give meaning to one's day-to-day work, that is, it should point into the future beyond one's daily work activities. It should motivate the individual to make a targeted and committed effort. A prerequisite for this to happen is that we are able to identify with the vision. If this does not happen, the vision may work against its purpose, because it can result in frustration on the part of the individual.

The vision should also provide guidelines for the activities that are important to concentrate on and those that are of less importance.

When we have a clear idea of the components of the vision, then a clear purpose for the vision will have been established, and the individual will be able to adapt his/her activities so that the desired future can be created.

The components of a vision are:

- Knowing what you want
- Knowing why you want it
- Knowing how to achieve it
- Knowing what you are trying to achieve with what you want
- Creating 'the new'

A vision should also provide clear indicators of what is good and what is bad behaviour. It should also provide a clear consensus for everybody regarding the overall objectives. Furthermore, a vision should function in such a way that it initiates a questioning process, which focuses on the future picture of the situation.

The power of a vision lies in the fact that everyone understands that the future situation will be created by them. It also provides guidance to relevant alternatives and becomes the yardstick by which these are assessed. A vision should correspond to the mental models that the actors have about how the social reality functions.

Creating a vision is linked to being able to develop syntheses, as well as the ability to communicate this clearly. Preferably, this should be done in relation to a concrete image, but a simple metaphor or a clear model can also be used. The vision should be clear, attractive and achievable, so that the creation of 'the new' is related to clear guidelines for daily activities.

Irritation Can Lead to Better Communication

If we have committed ourselves to a strategy, we will tend to positively evaluate the information that supports the strategy and overlook or underestimate information that goes against the strategy (Van Quaquebeke and Will Felps, 2018).

People prefer leaders who are consistent (keeping to a steady course) rather than leaders who change course frequently. Leaders also wish to portray themselves as being consistent (Thompson 1991). This can lead to leaders keeping to a steady course, even though it is not rational in relation to the most recent information; we can term this the 'steady course paradox'. Although the best choice for the system is to change course and relinquish previous commitments, the leader will gain more support (in the short term) if he/she keeps to a steady course, and thus appears consistent, although the course may be irrational in the current situation.

The 'steady course paradox' implies that systems should develop information and communication systems that reward the 'devil's advocates', i.e. those people who can argue against an established position (Janis 1982).

Creativity Involves Closing the Door to Memory

It is important to be aware that the starting position has a strong impact on the perception of the possible results. At a later point in the communication process, e.g. an original offer will function as a point of reference. The starting position is often the anchor chain that communication revolves around. Information is obtained in relation to this starting position. A good deal of research supports the hypothesis that the starting position is crucial to the end result (Baron 1990). For example: The price that you are willing to sell a house for is related to the price you originally think it is worth.

Both the communication and management literature emphasize the importance of setting and maintaining goals. However, this should not be confused with the idea that the goals are fixed; of course, goals may be subject to change as the process evolves.

Setting specific, challenging goals improves communication. Goals control what we are willing to accept and what we believe is achievable. However, setting unreachable or unrealistic goals can hamper the communication process.

When searching for further information, we tend to search those areas where we already have good knowledge, and not the areas where our knowledge is lacking; in other words, accessibility seems to have greater weight than relevance (Adriaenssen and Johannessen 2016).

If we have set a goal and we see that we are not reaching it, why do we tend to keep to the goal instead of changing course? The following points offer some explanations regarding this question:

1. We have difficulty distinguishing between past decisions and possible future decisions related to the past decisions. This is especially true when negative signals about the past decisions are presented.
2. We tend to rate positive information higher than negative information in relation to our original decision.
3. We tend to actively search for positive information that supports the decision we have made.
4. We tend to selectively filter out information that does not support our initial decision.
5. We tend to pass on information to others that supports our original decision.
6. We want to appear as being consistent.
7. We tend to reward leaders with positive feedback if they keep to a steady course, but to a lesser extent, leaders who change course.
8. We are controlled by the psychological investment we have put into a project.

Case Letter: Madness Is a State of Disconnection from Everything Other Than the Rational

In several studies, being short of time has been shown to promote a lowering of demands, quicker concessions and more rapid agreement. The following is an example of where the parties' time horizon is considered to have been significant: When the United States and North Vietnam were set to negotiate an end to the Vietnam War, the North Vietnamese made the first move: they rented a building on a two-year lease. The reason for this two-year lease was the knowledge that a party who negotiates under time pressure is generally in a worse position.

Create a Boundary, Then You Will Get Walled in

An alternative to the rational game-theory approach is discussed below. This approach is based on three basic elements:

1. The parties' alternatives for negotiating a consensus.
2. The parties' basic interests.
3. The relative importance of the parties' interests.

Bottom line:
Before we get involved in a communication conflict, we should clarify to ourselves what we will do if we cannot reach agreement. This will be our bottom line, i.e. we will be prepared to accept anything better.

The parties' basic interests
Making clear to oneself the underlying interests of a position helps one to clarify what one is really seeking to achieve. The example regarding sharing an orange in Chapter 5 illustrates this.

The relative importance of the parties' interests
The relative interests of each communication theme should be made explicit, because then we can clarify which ones we can give in to and which ones we *cannot* give in to.

Filling a Space with Nothing

In a communication situation, it may be of use to pay attention to the following list of strategic components:

1. Make it clear to yourself what you want to achieve in the situation.
2. Do what you think is best, and count on the others thinking the same way.
3. Acquire as much information as possible before the actual communication situation starts.
4. Show respect for the opposing party.
5. You should not leave the other person feeling that they have lost, because it is a small world and eventually you might be confronted with your own previous behaviour.
6. Differentiate between different situations, i.e. which situations require collaboration and which situations require you to be competitive.
7. Take into account your own position, i.e. if you are not in a strong position, do not act as if you have lot of power and influence (and vice versa).
8. Although it may concern economic matters, remember that life is not all about money.
9. Think strategically, that is, what should be your next step.
10. Once the communication situation is over, review what you have learned and use it in the next communication situation you are involved in.

It Is Never Too Late to Have an Unhappy Childhood

'The prisoners' dilemma' is an example from game theory. It tells us: Two people will be best served by remaining silent, even though one of them could do better by confessing. 'The social dilemma' is like the prisoners' dilemma, but the scenario involves more than two people. The best strategy in the social variation of the prisoners' dilemma is what we could call a CI strategy, i.e.

1. Cooperate, and if this fails then,
2. Imitate at all times the foregoing steps of the party who did not cooperate.

In order for the CI strategy to be as effective as possible, it should be made absolutely clear to the other party that one will respond by acting with exactly the same behaviour as the other party exhibits at all times. The following are examples of areas where the CI strategy has been used.

- Price wars
- Advertising wars
- Arms race
- Internal budgeting misspending

The following characteristics are integrated in the CI strategy:

1. Avoid unnecessary conflict by cooperating as long as the other party cooperates.
2. Provoke the other party by copying their previous move.
3. Show 'forgiveness' after you have followed up the other party's move.
4. Be clear about your behaviour so that the other party can adapt to your pattern of action.

This is a productive strategy because it is more or less collaborative, and can result in a win-win situation for the parties involved. However, it is important to be explicit so that a destructive pattern does not develop on the basis of misunderstandings.

Recent research has shown that in situations where there is a chance that a cooperative action may be perceived as a competitive (aggressive) action, and where a competitive action may be perceived as cooperative, the optimal strategy is to be even more 'friendly' than in the CI strategy, namely what can be termed CCI strategy, i.e. cooperate, cooperate, imitate. The CCI strategy means that one does not 'punish' the other party until two rounds have elapsed after the opponent has breached cooperation. This is the 'forgiveness' rule in practice. Research shows that the CCI strategy is a better strategy than the CI strategy. In the simulated games that led to the CI strategy, the CCI strategy would have won if the programme had been submitted by those participating in the game, which it was not (Axelrod 1984; Dixit and Nalebuff 2010).

The CI and CCI strategy are only effective if the relationship is of longer duration. If the relationship is of short duration, it may be better to 'strike first'.

The mathematical results on which the CI strategy is based show that it is superior if and only if the interactions between the actors have a sufficient degree of probability to continue over time. This suggests that if the expectations of a termination of the interactions arise, then a change to a competition strategy will occur,

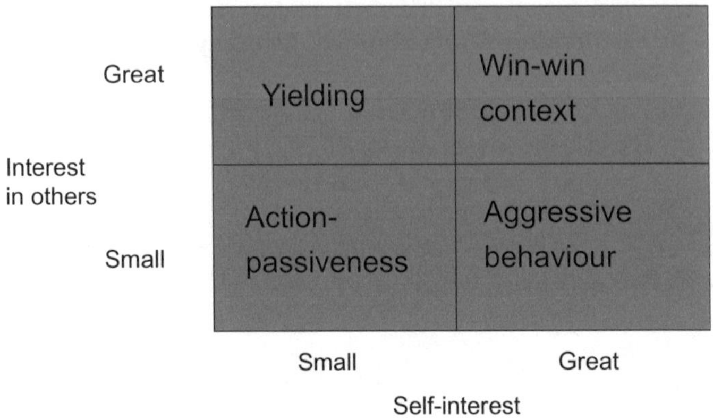

Fig. 10.2 Strategic communication behaviour

and will probably yield greater benefits to the party that acts first. On the other hand, if there is an expectation that the interactions will continue for a long time, where this has not been clear before, then the relationship could be transformed into a collaborative one, rather than a competitive one.

If the first of two parties in a collaborative situation inflicts loss on the second party, then this is referred to as an echo effect, i.e. it will really only be a matter of time before the 'boomerang' will return striking back at the first party.

In human interaction, however, it is not only self-interest that is at the forefront. Self-interest and interest in others exist along a scale from weak to strong.

If the interest in what results the others achieve is great, while the interest in our own results is small, then we will tend to be yielding.

If the interest in what results the others achieve is great, while the interest in our own results is also strong, then we will tend to strive for a win-win situation.

If the interest in what results the others achieve is small, and the interest in our own results is also small, then we will tend to exhibit action passiveness.

If the interest in what results the others achieve is small, while the interest in our own results is great, then we will tend to show aggressive behaviour.

We have shown these hypotheses in Fig. 10.2.

Knowledge of what interests a person has for their own results and the results of others can be used to predict how different people will behave in a communication situation.

Seven Influencing Techniques in Communication Situations

Seven influencing techniques have been identified in organizations in various communication situations. Below is an overview of these influencing techniques.

1. Reason: the use of facts and data to support a line of argument (e.g. I explained the reason for X occurring).
2. Alliances: mobilization of persons in the organization other than those directly involved in the negotiations (e.g. I got a, b and c to support me).
3. Flattery: using flattery, as well as making an impression on someone (e.g. He first told me what good leadership skills I had, and then he explained what he really wanted).
4. Bargaining: bartering, give and take (e.g. I offered them something in exchange, if they agreed to vote for our candidates).
5. Pressure: for instance, using power (e.g. I required that he did X).
6. Appeal to someone in authority: for instance, getting support from someone at a higher level in the organization (e.g. I was supported by boss X).
7. Sanctions: use of organizational rewards and punishments (e.g. I suggested higher wages, if–).

There Can Be No Order Without Disorder

Increasing tension in a conflict situation *can* lead to a reduction in tension because:

This can cause the parties to see that genuine communication is the only solution

It focuses on who really benefits from the status quo.

The whole system perspective is put into focus, not just the perspective of one of the parties.

BUT:
There is also a possibility of escalation, i.e. the conflict getting out of control is high.

THEREFORE:
When the tension has increased

THEN:
Send signals concerning willingness to find flexible solutions.
Isolate the conflict so that it does not spread to other parts of the system.
Select a different person to propose a flexible solution to the problem, rather than the one who has contributed to the increase in the conflict tension.
Keep to your basic interests.

Exercises

1. Discuss the following statements:
   (a) It's what you are best at that will be your downfall.
   (b) How can we learn but not learn?
   (c) Learning to see is different from seeing.
   (d) Creativity is closing the door of the memory so it is only slightly open.
   (e) Create a boundary, then you will get walled in.
   (f) On a smaller scale, structure is similar to process.
   (g) Previous small changes are different from later sudden changes.
   (h) Common-sense is not always good sense.
   (i) There can be no order without disorder.
2. In what way can we say that method affects the result we get?
3. In what way can preconceptions affect what we perceive in new situations?
4. In what way will relationships in a system influence what is reported?
5. Based on your desired future, answer the following questions:
   (a) What do you want, i.e. what goals have you set yourself? Set up three goals in order of priority.
   (b) Why do you want this?
   (c) How will you achieve this?
   (d) What are you looking to achieve?
   (e) How much energy, in terms of time resources, will you use to achieve your desired future?
6. What is meant by: accessibility carries greater weight than relevance?
7. List examples from your everyday situation where using the CI strategy could have provided a better solution in a communication situation than the solutions you chose.
8. Based on the model in Fig. 10.2 in this chapter, analyse yourself and find out which cell you would place yourself in. Let another person in the group analyse you. Did he/she choose the same cell for you? If not, discuss what may be the reason for this. You should not show the others in the group your assessment of yourself, until someone else in the group has assessed you.
9. Take four examples from your own everyday life where someone has tried to influence you. Which of the seven influencing techniques mentioned above were used? Did they use any other influencing techniques, if so, which ones?
10. First test yourself and then let another member of the group test you in relation to the following questions. If deviations occur, discuss why this might be. What can the results of this test be used for?
    (a) I have a low, moderate, high level of confrontational skills.
    (b) I have a low, moderate, high level of stress-tolerance capacity.
    (c) I have a low, moderate, high capacity for developing trust.
    (d) I have a low, moderate, high level of adaptability.
    (e) I have a low, moderate, high level of focusing ability.
    (f) I have a low, moderate, high level of planning skills.
    (g) I have a low, moderate, high level of emotional intelligence in work situations.

References

Adriaenssen, D.J. & Johannessen, J-A. (2016). Prospect theory as an explanation for resistance to organizational change: some management implications. Problems and Perspectives in Management, 14, 2: 84–92.

Axelrod, R. (1984). The evolution of cooperation, Basic Books, New York.

Baron, R.A. (1990). Environmentally induced positive affect: Its impact on self-efficacy, task performance, negotiation, and conflict. Journal of Applied Social Psychology, 20: 368–384.

Dixit, A.K. & Nalebuff, D.J. (2010). The art of strategy, W.W. Norton, New York.

Janis, I.L. (1982). Group Think, Houghton Muffins, New York.

Luhmann, N. (1996). Social systems, Stanford University Press, Stanford.

Strugar-Jelača, M. (2018). Redefining the management roles: Response to digital networking and access to a large amount of information. Strategic Management, 23, 2: 42–49.

Thompson, L.L. (1991). Information exchange in negotiation. Journal of experimental Social Psychology, 27: 161–179.

Van Quaquebeke, N. & Will Felps, W. (2018). Respectful inquiry: A motivational account of leading through asking questions and listening. Academy of Management Review, 43, 1: 5–27.

Watzlawick, P. (2014). Pragmatics of human communication, W.W. Norton, New York.

Weick, K.E. (1979). The social psychology of organizing, McGraw-Hill, New York.

Influencing Techniques 11

Aims of this Chapter

1. To provide knowledge about various influencing techniques in communication situations.
2. In this chapter, the reader should reflect on the following concepts:
   Idealized system design, analogue thinking, contrast principle, consistency principle, reciprocity principle, scarcity principle, authority principle, consensus principle, liking principle and heuristic assessment mechanisms.

Without Differences, Nothing can be Created

Information analysis is related to reasoning ability and, more specifically, to reasoning that is driven by a purpose towards a goal. In short, this function may be said to consist of our problem-solving ability regarding carefully demarcated and well-defined problems, as well as problems that are not so carefully demarcated and well defined.

When conducting information analysis, we should have the available and relevant information and have identified our goal. In other words, we have to transform the information with the aim of achieving a goal. There are several well-known techniques and methodologies for transforming information towards goals. One such methodology that the research literature has only addressed to a small extent is Ackoff's 'idealized system design' (Ackoff 1981). This methodology is concerned with identifying what a current system will look like in the future, i.e. an idealized design. Using available knowledge, it is then possible to work backwards from the assumed ideal future system. In this process, we should constantly focus on the crucial decision points that the system may have to consider. We then seek to plot a course in the present, to avoid problems that might occur at these future

K. Ledingham et al., *Rethinking Innovation*,
https://doi.org/10.1007/978-3-031-40848-9_11

decision points, which may lead to negative consequences for the system. In this way, it becomes easier to gain an overview of what problems need to be solved at given points in time, and what new information we will need to make rational choices. With the new information, we will have the opportunity to register the signals in time. Otherwise, these signals could easily have been overlooked, if we had not focused on precisely these possible future events. Ackoff's idealized system design is very similar to what Weick (1979) refers to as 'future perfect thinking', which can be used at different system levels, e.g. individuals, groups, organizations and society.

In the case of problems that are not so well defined, several methods are described in the research literature. One approach that has received attention is reasoning using analogies. This involves using previous knowledge, or newly acquired knowledge, related to a completely different problem area than the one we are seeking to solve. We attempt to see if there are relationships between the two problem areas. If such relationships exist, we study how solutions were found in the problem area that we are using analogously. We then see if it is possible to transfer solutions to the problem we are working on. We proceed in this manner until we find the solution to the problem in question.

Linking Information in New Ways Can Generate Creativity

Cialdini writes about six principles of persuasion that guide our everyday behaviour, in terms of influencing and being influenced by others (Cialdini 1993). These principles are: reciprocity, scarcity, authority, consistency, liking and consensus. In addition, Cialdini mentions a principle of human perception, the contrast principle, which can also be used as a tool of influence (ibid).

We will briefly review these principles to the extent that they are relevant to information analysis in communication situations.

The contrast principle:
If information that would have seemed negative if presented in isolation is preceded by other information that is unwelcome, then we have a tendency to overvalue the second piece of information. This principle can be used in many situations to make something more palatable than would have been the case if it had been presented either first or in isolation.

Case Letter: A Letter Home

For example: A female student writes home to her parents that she has been run over and taken to hospital. Her leg will have to be amputated, but otherwise she is healthy and in good spirits. Moreover, she writes that the doctors have discovered that she is pregnant. Also, the father found out through a routine blood test that he was HIV positive, although the doctors still haven't been able to confirm the

HIV status of the foetus. Finally, she writes that everything she has already written is untrue, but it was written to put the following information in perspective: 'I've failed my communications module at university, and so I'm coming home early'.

How do you think her parents will react to the information about her poor grade in communications?

The reciprocity principle:
If we receive something *before* we have to give anything, then we have a greater tendency to give in return. In the literature, this principle is often referred to as giving away free information.

Case Letter: Creating Reciprocity

For example: Before we send out a questionnaire to companies, we have found that if they first receive a short article telling them something useful about a project we're working on, together with a phone call in which we tell them about the project, then the response rate is far higher than if we simply sent out the questionnaire and asked companies to send it back as soon as possible.

The consistency principle:
As soon as we've made a choice, or adopted a position, we will experience personal psychological pressure, as well as pressure from those around us, to behave in accordance with our choice or the position we adopted.

Case Letter: Obligation

The socio psychological explanation for the consistency principle lies in our sense of obligation. In other words, if we can make someone feel obliged by taking up a position quite casually, then we can bind them by applying the consistency principle. Several techniques are employed to make people feel a sense of obligation. For example: Start very small and then build constantly on the pre-existing sense of obligation. Getting someone to say that they might *perhaps* agree to be interviewed can be the first step towards a whole sequence of research on a problem area. For the person who receives the request, this implies: If you don't want to get involved in an interview, then don't respond positively to the most trivial requests.

A second technique is to get the person to write down their obligations, or even to fill out an agreement. We tend to feel more obliged to keep to what we have written down ourselves than if others have written it, even though one is not more legally binding than the other.

A third technique is to get people make their views known to others. Once this is done, the person's actions will tend to be consistent with the point of view they had made known.

A fourth technique is to make people feel that the proposal actually came from them, while in reality it was another person's original suggestion.

However, adhering to the consistency principle can lead to the problem underlying the decision no longer being subject to critical scrutiny; that is, the sequence of actions can easily become automatic.

The consensus principle:
This principle expresses that we perceive something is true, because other people believe it to be true. If we present something as a generally held belief or opinion (consensus), then it is more probable that other people will accept it as a general truth.

The consensus principle has the greatest effect on people who are insecure about themselves, in ambiguous situations and when uncertainty prevails.

The liking principle:
We tend to agree with people we like, such as people we find physically attractive, rather than agree with people we find less attractive. The information presented by these people will be given more credence, even though the knowledge they present is not particularly insightful.

Case Letter: Familiarity

This principle also extends beyond physical attractiveness. It also applies to people with talent, or who are generous, honest or intelligent. By possessing, or by presenting oneself as having, some of these traits, individuals are more likely to make an impact when they present their views and thus possibly change our attitudes.

Furthermore, we tend to like people who are similar to ourselves, and we are more easily convinced by them.

This principle also has relevance when we know or have contact with the people concerned. It is also inherent in the extension of this principle that if we can get people to identify with the object or person to whom the information relates, then it will be easier to get the message across.

The authority principle
Information that is presented by an agency or person that holds a position of authority will be given more weight and be more likely to influence us than other types of information.

Case Letter: Obedience

The Milgram experiments (2010) demonstrated the principle of authority. In brief, study participants were led to believe that they were inflicting electric shocks to other people resulting in physical pain. A high proportion of the study participants obeyed the authority figure, who instructed them to perform the acts, exposing the other person to what they thought was great physical pain. In reality, the other person did not feel any physical pain, as the electric shocks were fake.

Milgram's explanation is that through systematic socialization processes, people learn to obey other people who hold positions of authority.

Furthermore, symbols of authority influence our behaviour. Research has shown that titles, clothing and things that give an aura of status and position have a strong impact on us, encouraging us to have confidence in the people who legitimize themselves through these symbols of authority (Cialdini 1993).

The scarcity principle:
People tend to value things more, if they believe availability is limited.

Case Letter: People Value What Is Scarce or Has Limited Availability

This principle expresses that people are more motivated to acquire something, if they think availability is limited, than if it is readily available. In other words, those things that are scarce are perceived as qualitatively better than those that are easy to obtain.

We react strongly to restrictions on our freedom, and especially on the freedom we have been able to achieve. If restrictions are placed on our access to information, our response will be the same as towards restrictions on the freedoms we have already acquired. We want more of this kind of information, and we tend to believe in it more.

One strategy for getting people to demand and believe more in one type of information may therefore be to have it censored in some way, e.g. excluded from public access, and then publish it subject to limited right of access. The same occurs if the government decides to exempt information from disclosure under the Freedom of Information Act. We tend to believe that this is valuable information. Moreover, should some information leak out, we believe more in the truthfulness of this information, than if the information had been made readily available.

Creativity Is Based on the Generation of Differences

It is very difficult to contest a line of thinking where the argumentation is logically consistent, but where the conclusion does not agree with the premises of the argumentation.

In the same way, it is possible to form erroneous statements based on a sound logical and coherent line of argument, **because** the premise for the argumentation may be incorrect. In the previous sentence, we use the word **because** intentionally, because it has been found that this word triggers a cognitive reflex, even though what follows the word does not always provide explanatory or more information (cf. Chapter 1).

What Is the Difference Between Information and Misinformation?

In our assessments of what information is most suitable in a situation, we often use rules of thumb (heuristic assessment mechanisms). The problem with heuristic assessment mechanisms is that we are not always aware that we are using them. Furthermore, using heuristic assessment mechanisms can lead to systematic errors in our evaluations.

There are four heuristic assessment mechanisms that we often use in everyday life. We make assessments based on:

1. Information that is currently accessible (recognition).
2. Information that comes most readily to mind (availability).
3. An initial value (anchoring).
4. Similarity (representativeness).

In the following, we will take a closer look at each of these heuristic assessment mechanisms.

Assessments based on information that is currently accessible
The information that is most visible is emphasized. For example: In advertising, it appears that frequency, i.e. the number of times something is presented, and the vividness, in the way it is presented, have great effect.

We tend to use the information that is readily available and overlook critical basic information. Critical basic information appears to be used when no readily available information exists. One explanation is that reviewing critical basic information is time-consuming and requires 'tedious' procedures, including the collection of basic data.

We use what is foremost in our memories (availability)
We have a tendency to attach more weight to information that allows itself to be retrieved most easily from our memories, than to information that doesn't allow itself to be retrieved so easily.

The subjects of one experiment were asked two questions:

a) In a four-page short story, how many words do you think have seven letters and end in —ing?
b) In a four-page short story, how many words do you think have seven letters where the sixth letter is —n-?

The results showed that most people gave a higher number in response to question (a) than (b), even though this had to be wrong, because words that have seven letters and end in -ing also have n as the sixth letter. Accordingly, there is a very high probability that the answer to question b is a larger number.

The explanation for this error may be that it is easier to retrieve words ending in -ing from our memories than it is to retrieve words where n is the sixth letter, due to the high frequency of the suffix -ing.

As a general rule, we are not so good at recalling how we felt during an uncertain situation until the results of our decision materialize. In other words, we have a tendency to allow the results to strongly affect what we actually believed before the results were available.

Research results clearly show that knowing the results increases individuals' belief that these are precisely the results they would have predicted, even if they had not known the results. One explanation of this is that cognitively, it is the knowledge of the results that is prominent in memory, and thus helps to control the assumptions about what we 'believed' prior to an event.

We should take note of the fact that so-called 'hindsight' is often informed by the results we already know, and not by what we actually thought prior to an action or event. Hindsight is different from learning from the mistakes we make. Moreover, when we evaluate other people's knowledge of a field, our own knowledge may influence how we evaluate them. Another consequence is that too much information, e.g. result information, can impair our assessment ability, because the results provide guidance for our assessment.

Assessments based on an initial value (anchoring)

A general rule of statistics is that a sample should be large enough compared to a population. However, this general rule does not seem to govern our intuitive understanding of phenomena.

Of course, the extreme case is when we generalize from a few individual cases and then state this to be a universal truth. Being caught out by 'the law of the small numbers' not only applies to laypeople, but also to scientists, leaders, lawyers, etc.

We often seem to be more convinced by our own experiences based on a small sample, 'I've experienced that myself', than if we are presented with a research result based on research that has been properly conducted.

Several studies have shown that people become fixated on clearly irrelevant information and take this as a starting point in their further assessments. In many cases, final decisions are systematically drawn towards this initial information—giving it undue emphasis in the final assessment.

Moreover, when people's knowledge of a specific area is reduced over time, their confidence in their own judgement of that area is not reduced to the same degree.

We compare with similar cases

We have a tendency to evaluate all information in the light of previous results and expect these results as a general rule to recur. We also have an unfortunate tendency to overestimate the probability of events that are linked and underestimate the probability of events that occur independently of each other.

When two events are linked, one assumes that the probability of them occurring is greater than if the events were not linked. However, it would actually be more logical to assume the opposite.

Example 1:
The findings of a study showed that experts thought it was less likely that:

1. Diplomatic relations between the United States and the Soviet Union would be severed in 1993 than that
2. A Soviet invasion of Poland would lead to the severing of diplomatic relations between the United States and the Soviet Union.

NB: One could of course have envisaged that the Soviet Union might invade countries other than Poland, leading to a severing of diplomatic relations, and so this suggests that scenario 1 was more probable than scenario 2.

Example 2:

a) A tsunami in North America at some point during 1989, resulting in the deaths of 1,000 people, was considered less probable than.
b) An earthquake in California that would trigger a tsunami resulting in the deaths of 1,000 people.

We tend to review all information in the light of past results and expect these results to have the most relevance. We also tend to overestimate events that are interconnected and underestimate events that occur independently of one another.

An elementary level of reflection ought to suggest that scenario (a) is more likely to occur than scenario (b), since b) is included within (a), and scenario (a) could occur due to many other causes.

At different times in a communication process, ask yourself the following questions: Is your reasoning now based on a previous decision, which forces you to proceed, or is your reasoning based on your basic priority interests?

What will the other person do if results are not achieved? It may be crucial for you to know what the other person will do in such a situation.

Exercises

1. Discuss the following statements:
   a) Without differences, nothing can be created.
   b) Linking information in new ways can generate creativity.
   c) Creativity is based on the generation of differences.
   d) What is the difference between information and misinformation?
2. Give an example of how the contrast principle can be used to influence others.
3. Give an example how the reciprocity principle can be used to influence others.

4. Give an example of how the consistency principle can be used to influence others.
5. Give an example of how the consensus principle can be used to influence others.
6. Give an example of how the liking principle can be used to influence others.
7. Give an example of how the authority principle can be used to influence others.
8. Give an example of how the scarcity principle can be used to influence others.
9. Give an example of how the word ‘because’ can trigger a cognitive reflex in another party.
10. What is meant by the fact that we are socialized into using linear causal thought patterns? Find two examples of this from your everyday life.
11. Give two examples of each of the following heuristic assessment mechanisms.
    a) We use the information that is currently accessible.
    b) We assume an initial anchor point (value).
    c) We compare to similar cases.
    d) We use the information that comes most readily to mind.

References

Ackoff, R.L. (1981). Creating the corporate future: Plan or be planned for, Wiley, London.
Cialdini, R.B. (1993). Influence: Science and practice, HarperCollins, New York.
Milgram, S. (2010). Obedience to authority, Pinter & Martin, London.
Weick, K.E. (1979). The social psychology of organizing, McGraw-Hill, New York.

Alternative Communication Strategies

12

Aims of this Chapter

1. To gain insight into why we believe more in one type of information than another.
2. In this chapter, the reader should reflect on the following concepts: emotional information, concrete information, 'local' information, the reference object, consensus information, conflict information and the cognitive value of information.

A Mink Does Not Gain More Freedom by Being Moved to a Bigger Cage

Information, say Nisbett and Ross (1980: 45–51), stimulates and holds our attention when it:

(a) Appears emotionally interesting
(b) Is concrete and provocative
(c) Is spatially and temporally close.

Information concerning people with whom we are emotionally linked will affect us more strongly than information about people with whom we do not have such a relationship. This factor can be used in a communication context by personalizing information, i.e. connecting any consequences directly to people with whom the other party has a close relationship.

Information relating to people with whom we have an emotional connection will influence us more strongly than information about people with whom we have no such connection. This can be exploited in a communications context by

K. Ledingham et al., *Rethinking Innovation*,
https://doi.org/10.1007/978-3-031-40848-9_12

personalizing information, i.e. by linking possible consequences directly to people with whom the other party has a close connection.

Information that is specific and supplemented with additional, vivid details will influence us more strongly than information about the same incident that is presented in a neutral fashion. If the words we use to present our information cause the other person to think about what we have told them in visual terms, this will reinforce an exhortation to them to undertake a specific course of action. We can achieve this by telling anecdotes, stories and case histories that bring the information we want to communicate to life, in contrast to relating generalized information of a more statistical nature. One example is the campaign against Norway's whaling industry. Opponents of whaling have succeeded in promoting an image of an intelligent creature capable of feeling emotions, on a par with those of a primitive human, swimming in majestic solitude through its primeval ocean. By anthropomorphizing whales, anti-whaling campaigners have been more successful in winning over public opinion than the pro-whaling lobby, with their statistics about whale numbers being sufficient to permit sustainable whaling. How does it help to show that whale numbers can sustain whaling, if people are picturing the hunting of a human-like creature? A similar example is the campaign against Norwegian seal hunting. When anti-hunting campaigners succeed in presenting seal pups as sweet little 'babies', this triggers a protective instinct in most people. Similarly, the information that one-third of the world's population is starving has far more impact on us when accompanied by an image of a child in a rubbish tip competing with rats for a mouldy piece of worm-eaten bread.

We are more affected by information which is spatially or temporally close to us, such as current local news, than by similar information about something that happens further away. For instance, news that the local church has burnt down would probably have a stronger effect on us than if several churches had burnt down in a foreign country.

In the context of negotiation, *emotional, concrete and 'local' information* can have an impact on the outcome of a communicative situation. In addition, it is reasonable to assume that linking these three aspects of information will have a greater effect than only a single aspect. Further, it is reasonable to assume that the longer we manage to direct people's attention to the information we present, and especially if it is related to the above three aspects, the greater the cognitive authority that the information will have, and the greater the likelihood that this will affect those people's assessment. This may be explained by the fact that their memory becomes more active. Moreover, on later occasions, they will be able to access this particular information from memory more easily when similar situations arise.

It should also be emphasized that it is not only accurate information that has this effect on us. Misinformation, for example, presented by the media, which is linked to the emotions, the concrete, or what is spatially or temporally close to us, will also affect us, and we will find it difficult to guard ourselves against both the information and our own reaction to it.

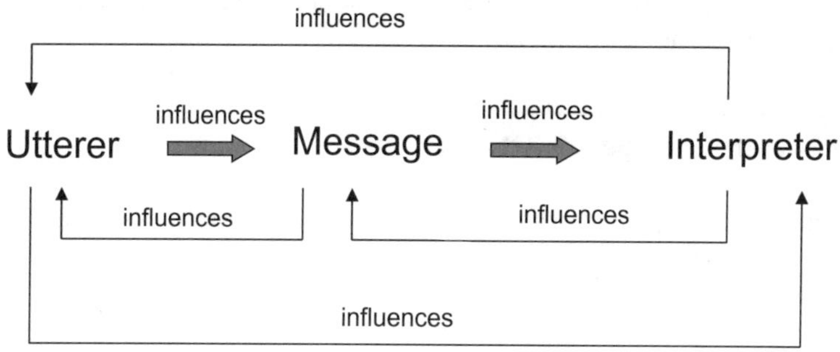

Fig. 12.1 Communication process

We Perceive the World Backwards

The supposition concerning why we believe more in one type of information than in another type is that it is the whole system: utterer, message and interpreter that should be taken into account.

We use the term interpreter rather than receiver, because interpreter reflects an active process, while the term receiver suggests a more passive activity. Figure 12.1 also attempts to show that the utterer (rather than sender) also affects the message. The utterer can also affect the interpreter. The message affects the interpreter, but it also affects the utterer.

Note that the message consists of three parts: information, relationship and hierarchy. The interpreter affects the message, and he she also affects the utterer.

The utterer (sender) has certain personal characteristics that affect us. The message also has certain characteristics that affect us. We as interpreters of the message contribute to attributing certain characteristics to both the utterer and the message that cannot be found either in the utterer or the information contained in the message.

It is reasonable to assume that information that supports our attitude towards a reference object will instil more confidence than information that disagrees with our attitude. A reference object is the object to which the information relates.

There is a strong connection between our attitudes and the confidence we have in the information about a reference object. What we do with this information is another thing, i.e. whether it causes us to act or not. In this context, it is our *confidence* in the information we are discussing here, not how we respond to it.

Numbers Are Different from Words, But They Become Words When They Are Spoken

An essential point in the relationship between attitude to the reference object and confidence in the information regarding the object is that the two elements can vary independent of each other. Attitude may vary in different contexts and at different times, but confidence in the information regarding the reference object will remain constant.

Case Letter: Change of Attitude

A person's attitude towards the use of alcohol may change, so he/she becomes more opposed to its consumption. Consequently, his/her confidence in information about the harmful effects of alcohol, in terms of both the physical and social consequences, will have gained a certain cognitive value. However, in some contexts and at certain times, it is conceivable that the individual in question consumes a certain amount of alcohol. In these contexts, it is most probable that he/she would have a more positive attitude towards the consumption of alcohol. Nevertheless, his/her confidence in information about the harmful effects of alcohol may still have the same cognitive value, even at times when his/her attitude towards alcohol has changed.

Information's Cognitive Value

The fact that we believe more in one type of information than another type, and that we manage to convince others to believe in the information, is linked to how we influence others. This may be expressed by the following question: Who says what to whom, through which channels, and with what effect? We can divide the question into the following elements:

- The one who utters the message
- The information
- The channel being used
- The receiver and interpreter of the message.

To date, there are no 'sociological laws' regarding the cognitive value of information. However, there are a good number of theories that can be used to gain insight into this phenomenon. The theories that were first launched were oriented towards three main variables:

- A focus on the information
- Understanding the content of the information
- The degree of acceptance of the information's conclusions.

Later research has greatly expanded the processes at work in relation to information and influencing. The following processes are considered important:

- Presentation
- Attention

- Agreement on the content
- Connections to previous knowledge of the persons
- Change in the behaviour of the recipient.

Extant theories express that if the information is to cause us to change behaviour, then all the processes in the above sequence should be operating correctly (Cialdini, 1993; Strugar-Jelača, 2018; Smorczewska, 2018).

Empirical studies have shown that two processes in particular are important. These concern capturing people's attention and making sure that content of the message is understood. Consequently, this means that the same type of information should be presented in different ways for different target groups. Simple and straightforward information may be suited to one target group, while more complex and well-reasoned information may suit another target group, although the content of the information is the same.

In recent research, heuristic theories have become popular. In brief, these have been oriented around the following:

- The sender's expertise; certification, i.e. the sender's educational background
- Context, i.e. the context of the information presented and received
- The personal characteristics of the sender
- The geographical location of the sender, i.e. where the sender resides
- The quality of the argumentation
- The background knowledge of the interpreter
- The relevance of the information to the interpreter
- How easy the information is to remember
- Subjective norms, i.e. the norms of the target group

(Holmes & Parker, 2016).

The different links between the above elements in different contexts and situations will determine the impact of the information presented. However, we do not know of any empirical studies that have examined all these elements and the relationships between them.

There Is a Difference Between a Description and What it Describes

One phenomenon that has emerged in group decisions is that groups tend to make decisions that are more extreme than the average of the individuals involved would have made. This may be explained by the fact that the group wishes to appear as having a clear and distinct identity. Further, if the group receives information about the decisions of other groups, the decisions of the group in question may be even more extreme. This indicates that information we evaluate independently will be assessed differently when we are in a group.

If what's around us changes slowly, we can almost always adapt
As a brief summary, we have developed the following rules regarding the confidence we have in information in a communication context:

- The temporal rule: The closer temporal proximity we have to an event or action, the more probable it is that the distortion of information is less than if the event or action happened longer ago.
- The spatial rule: The closer spatial proximity we have to an event, the more importance we will attach to it.
- The visual rule: If we observe an event with our own eyes, we will attach more weight to it than if someone else had described it to us.
- The first-hand information rule: If an event is communicated to us by someone who witnessed an event at first-hand, we will have more confidence in the information than if we were told about it by someone who was not present (second-hand information).
- The expert rule: We have more confidence in information presented by someone who is an expert in the field than by someone who is not.
- The status rule: We tend to have more confidence in information presented by someone who has a relatively high status and rank in society than by someone who hasn't.
- The 'facts' rule: We have a tendency to have more confidence in information that is documented with figures than information that isn't.
- The permanence rule: We tend to have more confidence in information that is of a more permanent nature than information that is of a temporary nature.
- The 'official stamp' rule: We tend to have more confidence in information that is exempt from the Freedom of Information Act than if the same information was made readily available.

Exercises

1. Discuss the following statements:
   (a) The dangers of mountain driving in an old Lada 4×4, and safety concerns.
   (b) We perceive the world backwards.
   (c) Numbers are different from words, but they become words when they are spoken.
   (d) There is a difference between a description and what it describes.
   (e) Interpretation occurs inside your head.
   (f) Analysis and synthesis are good neighbours, and good neighbours need good fences.
2. Give an example where information that is emotionally interesting, specific and close in time and space, can be used to capture someone's interest.

3. Give an example of a problem or phenomenon in everyday life where information is presented in an emotional way.
4. Based on a message you have recently received, analyse it in relation to its three components: a. the information component, b. its relational component and c. its hierarchical component.
5. How can a sender (utterer) directly influence the interpreter (receiver)?
6. How can a message directly influence the interpreter?
7. How can an interpreter influence the utterer (sender)?
8. How can an interpreter influence the message?
9. Find a news article in a daily newspaper written by a journalist. How is this news article related to:
    (a) The writer's expertise?
    (b) The context?
    (c) The personal characteristics of the writer?
    (d) The quality of the argumentation?
    (e) Your own background knowledge?
    (f) Your own norms about the phenomenon / problem that the news article focuses on?
10. Find a news article in a daily newspaper, and answer the following questions:
    (a) Does the information in the article support your views and attitudes or does it conflict with them?
    (b) Does the news article focus on news that has been in focus over a long period of time, or is it more recent (i.e. of a temporary nature)?
    (c) If the information in the news article supports your attitudes, would you say it has great or little value to you?
    (d) If the information in the news article goes against your attitudes, would you say it has great or little value to you?
    (e) Intuitively, does it correspond to your own opinions?
11. Based on the following rules regarding the confidence we have in information in a communication context, find examples from your everyday life where the rules have relevance:
    (a) The spatial rule (i.e. events that occur locally or far away)
    (b) The visual rule
    (c) The first-hand rule
    (d) The expert rule
    (e) The status rule
    (f) The 'facts' rule
    (g) The permanence rule
    (h) The 'official stamp' rule

References

Cialdini, R.B. (1993). Influence: Science and practice, HarperCollins, New York.

Holmes. W.T. & Parker, M.A. (2016). Communication. International Journal of Business Communication, 54, 1: 70–82.

Nisbett, R.E. & Ross, L. (1980). Human inference: Strategies and shortcomings of social judgement, Prentice Hall, Englewood Cliffs, NJ.

Smorczewska, B. (2018). Leadership as the construction of one's own story. Australian Journal of Career Development, 27, 2: 81–87.

Strugar-Jelača, M. (2018). Redefining the management roles: Response to digital networking and access to a large amount of information. Strategic Management, 23, 2: 42–49.

The Pragmatics of Communication

13

Aims of this Chapter

1. To gain insight into how a communication situation can be framed to maximize impact.
2. In this chapter, the reader should reflect on the following concepts : Thomas theorem, premise of action, utterance and mental constructions.

A Person Who Describes Something, Ignores Something Else

In communication contexts, it is crucial that we understand what situation we are in and how it is expected that we will act in the situation. In this way, the situational framework is also closely linked to how the actors in a communication process define their social world. '*If men define situations as real, they are real in their consequences*'.[1] This is the so-called Thomas theorem. In other words, how we interpret a situation will determine how we act in a situation.

The point is that we present different aspects of ourselves to others. In other words, it is only with a part of ourselves that we enter into social relationships. It is how relevant a person thinks the situation is, as well as the person's ideas and views that make up two important elements when defining a situation. There are numerous social realities that can appear to a person, which he/she has to frame in some way or other, and determine the status it has for him/her.

It is always the meaning we attach to our experiences that will form the framework for the situation we enter into. What we try to do in situational framing is to elicit some of the underlying processes that determine a communication situation.

[1] https://en.wikipedia.org/wiki/Thomas_theorem.

K. Ledingham et al., *Rethinking Innovation*,
https://doi.org/10.1007/978-3-031-40848-9_13

It is of great importance for the outcome of a communication situation that we make our premises, assumptions and motives as explicit as possible. The point of making these explicit is that these elements also guide our actions. If we have not made these elements explicit, then some of our actions will be unclear. What we take for granted in a social situation may prove to be mechanisms that govern how we evaluate and act in a situation. If such underlying mechanisms, which we are not fully conscious of, are in operation, it is reasonable to assume that we will benefit by bringing them to light.

When we take such elements in a situation as given, we risk developing cognitive schemata, typologies, reference points, etc., which can strongly affect how we evaluate other people, without us being aware of the fact that such cognitive schemata, typologies, reference points, etc., are in operation.

It is one thing how we present ourselves in a situation, but it is another how we evaluate others when they present themselves in the same situation. The bottom line is that we construct the social world based on our experiences and the knowledge we have available (Smith, 2005). Thus, it becomes a circular process that is operating. That is, it is not the case that we receive impressions, signals, symbols, information, etc., from the social world, and then construct our image of this reality. It is rather the other way around. We form some perceptions and then we look for signs, signals, symbols, etc., which these perceptions harmonize with. In this way, we are able to maintain our cognitive schemata and preconceptions without new information challenging our past experiences. Understood in this way, the creation of social reality becomes a conserving process for each of us and inhibits innovation and creativity.

It is the action, or more correctly the interaction between the actors, that is the basic point of departure for the situational framework.

Our Description of Something Will Always Be Different from the Thing We Describe

An utterance may be viewed in relation to three themes. These are rituals, the participant's close surroundings and how the utterance is 'wrapped in'. Rituals are linked to body movements, the person's appearance and the use of voice, all of which may be viewed as 'by-products' of the actual utterance, but nevertheless by-products that have a bearing on the utterance. The close surroundings refer to the people who are in the immediate vicinity of the person who makes the utterance and who are in some way or other connected to the utterance. 'Wrapping in' refers to whether or not the utterance originates from the individual who makes the utterance, or whether he/she is referring to the utterance of another.

Our Social Reality Differs from How We Describe It

Social 'facts' do not exist objectively. They are mental constructions and consequently should not be confused with 'facts' in the sense of something that has an objective reality, so we *should never 'realize the (social) facts'* so to speak. That social facts do not exist objectively means:

1. The concepts that are used to describe social situations are mental constructions.
2. We can change the use and meaning of the concepts and thereby the meaning of the social reality to which they refer.

Case Letter: Illiteracy

The word illiteracy denotes an inability to read or write. This is the meaning we have assigned to this word. If we consider this concept at face value, it is an objective social fact that some countries have higher levels of illiteracy than others. Perhaps it is also an ordinary social phenomenon that increased industrialization reduces the level of illiteracy in a country. However, we can also incorporate a wider meaning into the concept of illiteracy: For example, if large parts of a country's population can read and write, but have difficulties comprehending the meaning and context of what they read and write, we could describe this situation by extending the concept of illiteracy to make it broader than is usually the case. We could say that some people are functionally illiterate, even though they can read and write. We are the ones who construct social concepts, and what they refer to; we can also modify or change these concepts, and by doing so, we will also modify or change social 'facts'.

Who Constructs Social Reality?

Social reality today is largely created by the media, newspapers, TV, social media, etc. The media uses various methods to construct this reality for us. Our understanding and the meaning of reality are therefore to some extent governed by the methods used by others to create this reality. Consequently, our understanding of reality and the methods used to construct reality are strongly interconnected. Thus, the methods used to construct reality also guide our thinking and actions in relation to this social reality.

One of the most distinctive features of modern life is how distant events and actions strongly affect our lives, thinking and actions. Today, the world has become 'smaller' and more woven together. However, it is less certain whether we have become that aware of the consequences of living in this 'smaller' world.

Exercises

1. Discuss the following statements:
   (a) A person who describes something, ignores something else.
   (b) Our description of something will always be different from the thing we describe.
   (c) Our social reality differs from how we describe it.
2. Describe a situation from your own everyday life where it is clear that the situation in its consequence becomes the way you define it.
3. What does it mean when we say that we attribute a certain meaning to our experiences?
4. What is meant by the following statement, 'What we take for granted in a social situation may actually prove to be mechanisms that govern how we evaluate and act in the situation?'
5. What do we mean when we say that social facts are mental constructions? Explain this with an example from your own everyday life.
6. What is meant by the following statement, 'the methods used to uncover (construct) reality guide our thinking and actions in relation to this reality?'

Reference

Smith, D. (2005). Institutional ethnography. A sociology for people, AltaMira Press, New York.

14 Communication and Trust

Aims of this Chapter

1. To provide an understanding of how trust is established in a communication context.
2. In this chapter, the reader should reflect on the following concepts:

Expectations, rumours, typologization, the 'Protestant character', the 'sauna communicative syndrome', authentic meetings and information's cognitive authority (ICA).

Predetermined Is Not the Same Thing as Predictable

The *expectations* we have of a person will affect how we react to their behaviour. If we trust them, then our behaviour towards them will reinforce this impression. However, if a different impression is created of the person, through rumours, gossip, or the like, then our behaviour towards them will also be different. Consequently, our attitude towards the person concerned will reinforce the behaviour we expect of them. In this way, rumours and prejudice become mechanisms that trigger precisely the behaviour we expected, so we obtain a kind of affirmation of what we already 'knew'. This applies even if our expectations had no real basis. Accordingly, our expectations about another person have their own power, and rumours are more than mere innocuous information. Rumours and expectations both contribute to creating an image of a person that reflects the one that rumours encouraged us to imagine in advance. We could think of this as rumour running in advance and laying out garments that the person is required to put on, whether he likes it or not. Taking off these garments is an extremely difficult process. Accordingly, participating in spreading rumours is not a trivial matter. At best, it

K. Ledingham et al., *Rethinking Innovation*,
https://doi.org/10.1007/978-3-031-40848-9_14

embodies poor judgement and ignorance, and at worst, it is done deliberately to damage another person.

The prior knowledge we have about a person also has the same weight as the expectations and rumours we have about a person. This prior knowledge and our expectations sometimes hinder the other person from communicating in a situation. We use past experience of similar 'types', and then, we judge the person in question on the basis of our own typology. In other words, where there are other 'similar' people that we know that determines how we behave towards the person we know nothing about. Once we have entered a person into our 'register of types', he/she will be trapped in a kind of informational fox trap, and like a fox will have to free himself by gnawing off his own leg.

Another way of thinking about this is to imagine a situation where we have no advance information about a person. This causes us to run around in our own heads like confused metaphorical chickens, gobbling up all the available information that might possibly allow us to categorize this new person as one of the types we have randomly created on the basis of other, similar people. If the person does not behave in the way our typologies lead us to expect, then we react with disquiet and uncertainty, and behave towards the person in a negative way.

We are extremely limited in our willingness to allow others to put their own case in a social situation. We take on the role of missionary, even if we have never been inclined to that calling. And the message we evangelize consists of typologies from our own narrow world of personal experience. In the case of this type of information, we can say definitively that evaluation comes before presentation.

Once we have formed an opinion about a person by applying our typologies, we have a tendency to overlook information that challenges this opinion, and we look actively for information that supports our established register of types. It is as though we have an inner hoarder who is working overtime to create order within an order that was already established. Although our inner hoarder finds information that challenges the established order that our typologies have created, he keeps it behind locked doors in dust-covered files, before possibly taking it out a later time for the purposes of self-justification: That was what we thought *actually*. Our inner hoarders seem to have real authority over most of us.

The more our typologies are informed by our earlier experiences, the more difficult it seems to be to change them. We find it difficult to change these typologies even though new information suggests that we should. One such typology is possibly a legacy of the Reformation and is what we might refer to as '*the Protestant character*'. We have a special fondness and trust in people who exhibit this kind of character. A person of Protestant character has great capacity for generating trust and authority. The character traits of this type of person are as follows: He (because the person is usually male) is a serious person, who does not smile in serious situations. For people with a Protestant character, most situations are serious. He embodies impartiality and distances himself as a general rule from the situation at hand. He observes, but seldom shows his feelings about a situation. You will seldom or never hear him utter an ironic comment, and laughter is almost sinful. He is reasonably well informed about most things, and as a rule expresses his opinions with a serious expression. He expresses opinions only about his own field and then with carefully balanced consideration. He supports fairness for all, but keeps his private life separate from this. His self-image is irreproachable, and he makes a convincing case for both sides of the argument, but as a rule comes to a conclusion that benefits his own side. The Protestant character promotes trust and is something we want to see in our public servants.

A feeling of freedom in social interaction is often dependent on us knowing something about the other person's position in the social hierarchy. In order to establish the position of the other person, we partake in what we can call the 'sauna communicative syndrome'. That is, in the opening gambits in conversations between two people who do not know each other, they often follow a sequence whereby each one metaphorically undresses the other, by requiring him to give his name, before quickly moving on to what the other does, i.e. his work, position and so on. What is of interest in these opening conversational gambits is not who you are, but where you fit within the social hierarchy. And if another person does not 'undress' us, then we quickly undress ourselves, even if only through a well-placed half-sentence. In this way, we become free to know what we can talk about. In the armed forces, the problem is solved by having stars on the shoulders of uniforms (the number of stars showing the rank). However, in civil life, we have to resort to other means to identify the social position of others. Consequently, we must conduct a so-called 'sauna manoeuvre', and when the social 'undressing' is finished, the conversation can start, as then we know what we can talk about, and most importantly, what we shouldn't talk about.

In a way, it is as though our opinion is communicated through what is left unsaid, in the same way as the part of a doughnut that can't be eaten is what makes a doughnut a doughnut.

The Authentic Meeting

Building trust is crucial to establishing an effective communication environment. A verbal model for building trust is described below.

In a 'meeting' (or an anticipated 'meeting') with new actors, there will be a need to reduce the uncertainty (or anticipated uncertainty) that the actors bring to the interaction. Clarifying and defining the reciprocity that must exist between the actors will be an important factor that can facilitate an 'authentic meeting', i.e. a meeting where the actors are honest with both themselves and the other party.

Reducing uncertainty can be achieved by means of the repetition of certain actions, provided that these positively reinforce interaction. When such positive reinforcing loops work over time, they will also contribute to creating an 'authentic meeting', thus reducing uncertainty between the actors.

In order to reduce uncertainty, the repetition of positive actions and reciprocity should have a strong moral and emotional aspect. This emotional dimension will strongly introduce the 'personal' element into the interaction, which may be regarded as an absolute prerequisite for establishing an 'authentic meeting'.

The moral dimension should function in such a way that it explicitly illuminates the actors' premises, assumptions and motives. This is to bring clarity into the process, so that the actors know where they stand in relation to each other, which is an essential basis for establishing an authentic meeting. The moral dimension also introduces norms and values to the interaction. Clarifying these elements is important in the trust-building process. The moral dimension also concerns the requirement for value consistency between intentions, means and goals. These three elements should be subjected to a value analysis, precisely because people learn and acquire habits over time, which in turn develop into ideas that guide our way of thinking and acting, but of which we are not necessarily aware.

Integrating a significant part of the actors' identities into the interaction diminishes the meeting's calculative and strategic aspect. Although both parties enter into the meeting from a strategic perspective, it is not such a utility aspect that creates the necessary trust. The economic benefits, on the other hand, are a result of the trust-building processes having worked over time and are not a prerequisite for this. If the actors mainly act on the basis of a view of humanity as driven by self-interest, and incorporate this idea into their models, they may end up with their premises being laid bare, leading to the results that will follow from this.

In order for reciprocity and the moral dimension to play an active role in the trust-building processes, it is crucial that the interaction is not based on a power relationship of 'master and servant'. Mutual trust will not be able to exist in such a context, and an authentic meeting will thus not be constituted. If one employs a type of strategic behaviour that only exploits other people to achieve goals, then this will be contrary to the reciprocity requirement and the moral dimension. However, if one employs a type of strategic behaviour that is based on reciprocity, then this may develop into spontaneous friendship. Such strategic behaviour involving spontaneity and authentic meetings also provides a potential for positive change, something we should not overlook in the daily practical reality.

One distinctive characteristic of trust processes is that it takes time to generate trust, while the breach of trust can occur quickly. Breaching a moral requirement can trigger a critical threshold for the entire trust-building process. Even if the breach takes place in a completely different place in the network than the part focused on, it may have negative consequences for the entire network. The reason for this is probably that although trust processes operate in the daily practical field, they are based on such basic human elements that if these are subject to exploitation, the breach of trust will be a fact.

There does not appear to be symmetry in the building-up of trust. One party normally takes the lead in initiating the process. Symmetry only occurs at a later stage, when trust has been established as an active factor.

What We Know Is Different from What Is Facts

Why do we have more faith in one person than another? Does someone's appearance have significance for the trust and confidence others have in them? Most people would probably not like to be confronted with the idea that someone's attractive appearance might influence the extent of trust they have in them. Of course, attractiveness is culturally and historically determined. Nevertheless, this does not alter the idea that attractiveness influences the trust people have in others. Attractiveness is also dependent on the image we present to others, and consequently, the trust and confidence we create in others are also dependent to a certain extent on how we present ourselves.

There will always be certain thresholds that we must cross before our trust-building ability is damaged. However, if we exceed these limits, then unfortunately, we will have to do a great deal more on other fronts in order to re-establish our image of credibility as someone who inspires confidence. It seems reasonable to assume that someone that exhibits certain 'Protestant characteristics' may allow themselves more leeway, before trust in them is shaken, than a person who does not possess such characteristics.

It should also be emphasized that in addition to culture, context and situation are also important; nevertheless, aesthetic mechanisms in relation to trust-building abilities are also at work here. Furthermore, our assessments change over time; but in this context, this is not of interest, as it is always in the here and now that we assess how a person appears, even in the case of historical persons.

It may seem as though there is a balancing mechanism in operation to adjust for the fact that appearance is significant for a person's ability to generate trust, in that popular wisdom has given rise to the following expressions: 'all beauty but no brains'; 'handsome but empty-headed'; 'fast feet, slow head'. The expression 'all beauty but no brains' can be explained by the fact that we have the fundamental idea that everyone is created equal, and if some are more equal in some ways, then they must be less equal in others.

As mentioned, few people would like to admit that someone's appearance influences the degree of trust and confidence they have in them. However, several studies have shown that appearance does influence the confidence we have in people, and consequently, how we behave towards them (Cialdini 1993). It should also be emphasized that the research findings are not entirely clear; we may also have negative biases towards attractive people. But on the whole, this does not seem to be the case; the courtroom provides an example of a situation in which our credibility is certainly at stake. However, even here, where one would presume that law and justice prevailed, research has shown that a person's appearance, dress and behaviour are important and can affect the outcome of a case (Dermer and Thiel 1975).

An important point here is not only how the other person presents himself/herself, but how we present ourselves to the other person. Self-understanding and status act upon each other. By self-understanding, we mean how we perceive ourselves in relation to others. By status, we mean how the other person perceives us. Status is created to a certain degree in relation to one's self-understanding. Status is also created through communication with others. Our assessments will often be based on self-understanding and status.

If we invest effort in how we appear to others, will this have any relevance for our credibility? The answer seems to be a clear yes, as is evident from many research reports, but within certain limits (Dion et al. 1972). If we go beyond these limits, this may have a boomerang effect with regard to people's confidence in us. The rule here is perhaps: It is important to appear as 'average'. However, most of us are above or below this 'average'. Nevertheless, in most cases, it will help our credibility if we attempt to appear as 'average'. Thus, it is not always best to *be oneself*, but rather to appear in the eyes of others as being 'average'. This may seem like a paradox in terms of creating trust and confidence. On the one hand, we tend to trust people who are themselves, but we do not have full trust in them if they are above average, although they are 'being themselves'. This may be one explanation for why someone with a so-called 'Protestant character' often has a good trust-building ability.

Invention Is Not the Same as Discovery

Information's cognitive authority (ICA) is a concept we use here, which refers to the idea that we tend to believe more in one type of information than in another type.

Information's cognitive authority concerns the relationship between two people and is related to the fact that the degree of cognitive authority will always vary. Further, information's cognitive authority is related to areas of interest.

Figure 14.1 illustrates how information's cognitive authority (ICA) is linked to competence and confidence.

Figure 14.1 shows that if we have low confidence in a person, but he/she has a high level of competence in the area in focus, then we will attribute a moderate level of cognitive authority to the information.

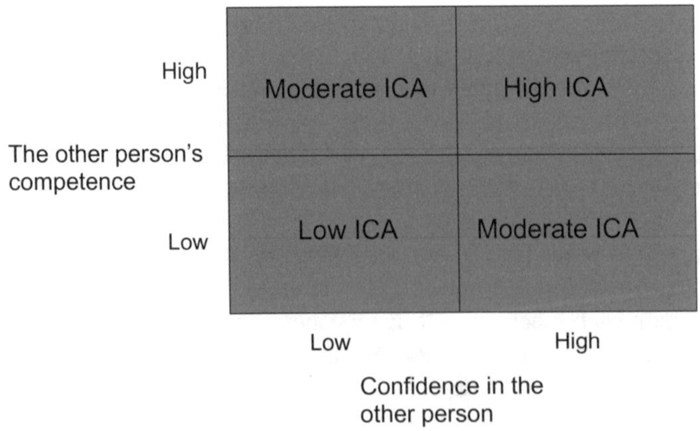

Fig. 14.1 Confidence and competence

If, on the other hand, we have a high level of confidence in the person, and he/she has a high level of competence in the area in question, then we will attribute a high level of cognitive authority to the information.

If we have low confidence in the person and he/she has a low level of competence in the area in question, then we will attribute a low level of cognitive authority to the information.

However, if we have a high level of confidence in the person, but he/she has a low level of competence in the area in question, we will attribute a moderate level of cognitive authority to the information.

Exercises

1. Discuss the following statements:
   a) Predetermined is not the same thing as predictable.
   b) When we are aware of the consequences of our behaviour, we can change our behaviour.
   c) What we know is different from what is fact.
   d) Invention is not the same as discovery.
2. How can the expectations we have of a person contribute to the image we have of him / her? Give some examples from your own everyday life.
3. How can rumours about someone contribute to creating the behaviour we expect him / her to have? Use examples from your own everyday life.
4. What is meant by the statement: 'We are extremely limited in our willingness to allow others to put their own case in a social situation?'.
5. What does it mean when we say 'the evaluation comes before the presentation?'.
6. List examples from your local environment of people that have a so-called 'Protestant character'. Add further characteristics to this phenomenon than those mentioned in this chapter.
7. List examples from a communication situation with a foreign person in which you have used the 'sauna manoeuvre' (described in this chapter), and examples where you have been subjected to the manoeuvre.
8. Give three examples of how the level of confidence one has in someone can affect a communication situation.
9. Discuss the statement: If the actors mainly act on the basis of a view of humanity as driven by self-interest, and incorporate this idea into their models, they may end up with their premises being laid bare, leading to the results that will follow from this.
10. Choose someone you know and answer the following questions:
    a) Does this person have a low or high level of competence in a particular field?
    b) Do you have a low or high level of confidence in this person?

How will the information on a topic that this person communicates to you influence you? Imagine that he/she first conveys something within his/her area of competence, and then imagine that he/she conveys something from an area of competence in which he/she does not have special expertise.

References

Cialdini, R.B. (1993). Influence: Science and practice, HarperCollins, New York.

Dermer, M. & Thiel, D.L. (1975). When beauty may fail. Journal of Personality and Social Psychology, 31: 1168–1176.

Dion, K., Berscheid, E. & Hatfield, E. (1972). What is beautiful is good. Journal of Personality and Social Psychology, 24: 285–290.

Communication and Values

15

Aims of this Chapter

1. To provide an understanding that a person in a communication situation conveys three things at the same time: their position, basic interests and values.
2. In this chapter, the reader should reflect on the following concepts:
   Basic values, basic interests, position, socialization process, mental variables and norm distribution.

Mastery Is Not the Same as Understanding

An individual's basic values are here considered as a multi-dimensional system. This values system permeates everything in an actor's social attitudes towards their surroundings. However, it is difficult to find out what a person's values system is. This is because we often omit parts of this system for various reasons when presenting ourselves in social situations. It may also be precisely what we omit to communicate that is the most pervasive element in the values system.

Of course, we usually express our values system in some way or other, but it is conceivable that it would benefit the other party most if they were familiar with what we do not communicate.

Furthermore, it is often the case that the values that are the most fundamental, even in a subtle way, guide how we perceive the other person, and thus, how we interpret their behaviour through our typologies. Obtaining information about the other's value system helps to create order in how we view the other person.

When we meet another person, we always assess them in one way or another. This assessment is based on our own experience. One technique for avoiding conflicts that can follow from such an assessment is to attempt to distinguish between

K. Ledingham et al., *Rethinking Innovation*,
https://doi.org/10.1007/978-3-031-40848-9_15

perception and assessment. Such a distinction will greatly influence our behaviour in relation to the other person, and in the way, we collect information about them.

The study of information is inseparable from the study of communication, and insight into our own as well as the other person's values system is crucial to information processes, because the values system is the most fundamental aspect of a communication process.

The values system cannot be subjected to hierarchical considerations without damaging it; that is, the values system will be forced into a straitjacket, where it will eventually be perceived by the actors as if it were hierarchical.

Being Bigger Than Is Not the Same as Being the Thing That Is Bigger

Instead of considering the goal the other person has, an equally important approach is to consider the values or norms that are inherent in a particular action that the person is performing. By gaining insight into the values behind a person's actions, we can uncover the pattern of values that he/she has, and thus be better able to understand the real motives he/she may have in the situation in question. The reasoning behind this approach is that people embed their whole philosophy of life into their everyday actions, and if we understand this, we will be able to understand their future actions (Smith 2005).

The Difference Between Order and Disorder Is the Amount of Freedom We Give Them

The mental variables that for some reason do not change value in a course of development have a tendency to become 'frozen'. Possibly, part of the explanation why extreme attitudes are established towards others, and one's basic values develop, may be due to the 'freezing' of some mental variables at an early stage.

Throughout the entire socialization process, some mental variables are kept stable, while others are given a greater degree of freedom to operate within. The variables that are kept stable then form our basic values, while the variables that have gained more flexibility give us the opportunity to develop our values base.

An investigation of the value base should therefore start by examining the mental variables of a culture that the socialization process has attempted to stabilize. This will also give us insight into the other person in a communication situation.

Borders Are Always Where Differences Can Be Seen

The development of group norms can control a communication situation. Examples of the norm distribution in groups are the following:

1. *Effort* is important.
2. It is *the results* achieved that are important.
3. It is the *commitment* you show that is the deciding factor.
4. It is the *principle of equality* (according to very specific criteria of equality) that is crucial.
5. It is *the needs* of the individual that are important.
6. It is what the person *has previously done* for the group that is the deciding factor.
7. One or other *combination of 1–6*.

In communication situations concerning the distribution of a resource, it is crucial that the group norms, especially the distribution norms, are made explicit. However, it is not easy to agree on a group's distribution norms; when the distribution norms are discussed and some form of agreement about which ones to follow are clarified, then this should be adhered to. If one often changes the distribution norms in a group context, it is reasonable to assume that unnecessary conflicts may develop, which can hamper both the creativity and efficiency of the system.

Exercises

1. Discuss the following statements:
   a) Mastery is not the same as understanding.
   b) Being bigger than is not the same as being the thing that is bigger.
   c) The difference between order and disorder is the amount of freedom we give them.
   d) Borders are always where differences can be seen.
   e) We are not our feelings, just as we are not our thoughts.
2. Set up two points representing the pillars of your values system. Discuss this with the others in the group.
3. What is the difference between perception and assessment of a particular everyday situation? Give at least three examples.
4. In what way is a values system crucial to a communication process?
5. What does it mean when someone views it as important for their human dignity to maximize certain human values?
6. Based on the following distributional norms, discuss what you think should be the norms basis of your workplace / school. Prioritize the distribution norms as you think they should be used:
   a) It is the intention that is important.
   b) It is the results achieved that are important.
   c) It is the commitment you show that is the deciding factor.
   d) It is the principle of equality that is crucial.
   e) It is the needs of the individual that are important.
   f) It is what the person has previously done for the group that is the deciding factor.

7. As your starting point, take a discussion you have had with a person at your workplace. Answer the following questions:

    Answer the following questions:
    What did you want to achieve?
    How did you want to achieve this?
    What did you try to change/maintain in the system?

8. Find values in the Norwegian culture that you believe have been stable over a long period.

Do you feel that these values say something about your own values?

Reference

Smith, D. (2005). Institutional ethnography. A sociology for people, AltaMira Press, New York.

The Effect of Being Positive 16

Aims of this Chapter

1. To provide an understanding of how emotions are regulated by the development of relationships between actors in a communication situation.
2. In this chapter, the reader should reflect on the following concepts:

Emotions, positive feedback loop, negative feedback loop and the 'Protestant character'.

Local Links Generate Collective Behaviours

Emotions are often linked to motivation. In this way, emotions can have an impact on behaviour. The expression of emotions may be understood in relation to the extent of commitment we attach to a particular situation. Emotions, like other broad concepts, are difficult to define, and there is no generally accepted definition of emotions, say Bowers et al. (1985: 501–502). However, we can examine the various expressions of emotion, such as anger, embarrassment, pride, joy and fear.

When we have no agreed definition of emotions, but need to explain the expression of the various emotions separately, we will eventually encounter difficulties, because the expressions of emotion can vary from culture to culture.

Most people would agree that emotions have a direct impact on our assessments of situations, and the actions we take. We usually tend to make a clear distinction between emotions on the one hand and rational thinking on the other hand. Popular sayings such as 'follow your heart' and 'use your head' illustrate this general contrast between emotions and rationality. In the majority of scientific fields and institutions, a distinction is made between rationality and emotions, in the sense that rationality negates emotions in the sense that the latter is not included in the various scientific approaches.

K. Ledingham et al., *Rethinking Innovation*,
https://doi.org/10.1007/978-3-031-40848-9_16

What we feel about a person will largely determine how we act towards that person. Consequently, it is reasonable, if not necessarily 'rational', to consider emotions and thinking as one coherent thought system. If we consider emotions and cognitive processes as a single system, it will not be fruitful to attempt to identify linear causes and effects, but more productive to view these elements as appearing in a circle, and in a circle there is no beginning or end.

Emotions are also directly linked to a relationship between one person and one or more other persons. Considered in this way, emotions become an integrated element in the system they are part of.

Case Letter: Changing Our Reaction to the Behaviour of Others

If A is aggressive towards B, this can cause B to socially reject A. When B socially rejects A, A's aggressive behaviour may be reinforced, leading to a conflict that can easily spiral out of control. This is an example of a positive feedback loop.

If we look at emotions in this way, it is not difficult to understand how emotions can affect the development of a relationship. By considering emotions from this point of view, we can then categorize the emotional expressions between two people, or groups of people as positive and negative feedback loops.

When positive feedback loops are in operation, a system will escalate and soon get out of control. If negative feedback loops are in operation, a balance can be achieved. An important point in viewing emotions in this way is that how we evaluate or interpret each other's emotions is important both with regard to our own reactions and also for the development of the other person's behaviour in the relationship. We also gain insight into the pattern that emotions help create and maintain by viewing emotions as interactions between two or more people.

Thus, in communication contexts, it is not so much the other person's emotional behaviour that is of interest, but rather how *we react* to the other person's emotional behaviour. In other words, we can directly regulate the other person's behaviour by regulating our own reactions to his or her behaviour.

The Future Determines the Present

In those situations where an expectation that something will happen, or an assumption that something will happen, the future may be viewed as determining the present, because an expectation by definition refers to the future. Understood in this way, a cause comes before an effect, but not necessarily following a linear direction of time.

Case Letter: The Expectation of a Price Increase Leads to a Price Increase

If the directors of the five largest oil companies state that they expect the price of petrol and oil to rise by 30% in the following month, this statement of expectation would probably lead to queues at the service stations the following day. In other words, it is probable that the price would rise as a result of the expectation expressed by the directors. Similar phenomena can occur at the personal level. If a person expects to be rejected, then he will behave in such a way that it is probable that he will be rejected.

An Unfamiliar System Will Be Described as Chaotic by the Ignorant

Positive and negative emotions can greatly influence a communication environment, and thus the outcome. Positive emotions are associated with greater generosity and helpfulness, as well as increasing the ability for creative problem-solving and reducing aggressiveness and suspicion (Bazerman and Lewicki 1983). Humour helps to curb suspicion in a tense communication situation. Perceived justice also helps facilitate the development of positive emotions. Several studies show that positive emotions reduce aggressive tactics while increasing the benefits (outcomes) for both parties (Bazerman et al. 1988). However, there is surprisingly little research that focuses on the importance of emotions in communication situations (Bendor et al. 1991). One explanation may be that it is difficult for researchers to observe and classify the emotions, and difficult to verbalize for those concerned. The socialization process may also dampen the behavioural expressions of emotions, so that the emotions are expressed differently in different cultures, making research even more difficult.

Before a professional communication situation begins, we should think about how we want to feel when it is completed; otherwise, from an emotional point of view, we may end up in a quite different situation than what is desirable.

When We See that Something Is Happening, Then It Has Already Happened

A good deal of research suggests that positive emotions facilitate problem-solving in communication contexts (Carnevale and Conlon 1987). The results of this research suggest that positive emotions have the following effects in communication situations:

- Positive effect on trusting others, and also improvements in the final results.
- Improving creative problem-solving ability.
- A greater tendency to create win–win situations.

• An improvement in the exchange of information in negotiations.

The contrast to positive emotions in a communication situation could be described as a distance from the expression of emotions, which takes place in any situation where people interact, and in particular when we are involved in conflicts. If distance is a contrast to positive emotions, then research findings indicate that what we describe as 'the Protestant character' is not well suited to conflict resolution. The explanation may be that even if we apparently have trust in people who possess these character traits, then there is an impression of manipulative behaviour that is implicitly present in the Protestant character.

The paradox is possibly that we have trust in the Protestant character, but we feel slightly uneasy in its presence, because in its immediate presence we notice the grasping for control, the manipulative force and the judgemental attitude to our own natures.

In other words, the Protestant character conveys a dual message: One is trust. The other is an implied force that is used as a domination technique, a kind of brutal suppression of others' spontaneity, diversity and emotional expression.

To sum up, we could say: What is good for a person with a Protestant character is also good for everyone else. For those who are not so accustomed to read between the lines, of course this statement is intended ironically and is the premise upon which people with a Protestant character operate.

Exercises

1. Discuss the following statements:
   a) Local links generate collective behaviours.
   b) An unfamiliar system will be described as chaotic by the ignorant.
   c) When we see that something is happening, then it has already happened.
2. Develop your own loop models for the following conditions. At least one model shall be developed for each of the points under (a-j)
   a) If A shows anger towards B, what will B's reaction be?
   b) What can B do to reduce A's behaviour?
   c) If A feels embarrassed on behalf of B, how do you think B will respond if he/she is aware of this?
   d) How can B change A's feelings and how can A change B's behaviour?
   e) If A expresses happiness to B how do you think B will respond?
   f) How can B effectively change A's expression of emotion?
   g) If A expresses fear towards B, how do you think B will react?
   h) How can B react to change A's fear?
   i) If A expresses arrogance towards B, how do you think B will react?
   j) How can B change A's behaviour?
3. What is meant when we say that people with a 'Protestant character' exhibit manipulative behaviour?

References

Bazerman, M.H. & Lewicki, R.J. (ed.). (1983). Negotiating in Organizations, Sage, New York.

Bazerman, M.H., Mannix, E. & Thompson, L. (1988). Groups as mixed-motive negotiations. In I.E.J. Lawler & B. Markovsky (ed.), Advances in group processes: Theory and Research, Vol. 5, JAI Press, Greenwich, Conn.

Bendor, J., Kramer, R.M. & Stout, S. (1991). When in doubt: Cooperation in the noisy prisoners dilemma. Journal of Conflict Resolution, 35: 691–719.

Carnevale, P.J. & Conlon, D. (1987). Time pressure and mediator strategy in simulated organizational dispute. Organizational behaviour and Human Decision Processes, 40: 111–133.

Communication and Punctuation 17

Aims in This Chapter

1. To gain an understanding of the fact that relationships are something more than only cause and effect chains.
2. In this chapter, the reader should reflect on the following concepts:
   Linear relationships, circular relationships, patterns, critical variables and sociological laws.

A Circle Becomes a Straight Line When Viewed on a Very Small Scale

In a communication context, Fig. 17.1 attempts to show that it is the scale we use when assessing a situation that influences the results we achieve. Further, the figure shows that the scale we use can give us input for either an understanding of patterns, by considering the whole circle, or excluding us from insight into the patterns that operate in a situation, by viewing a situation as a straight line (AB). When viewing the straight line, we focus on the linear relationship, while viewing the whole circle, we focus on the circular relationships.

Patterns concern how we as observers distinguish or create differences between variables. Some variables are referred to as critical, others as less important. The critical variables are then separated from a background, and in undergoing this process, create a pattern in the social sphere. Thus, the variation in a pattern becomes less than the variation in what we have defined as the less important variables.

Metaphorically, we can say that revealing a pattern may be compared to studying whirlpools in a river. To find the pattern in these whirlpools, we need to study them from different angles and at different places in the river. If, on the other hand, we take a linear starting point, we may lose sight of the pattern; it is the pattern

K. Ledingham et al., *Rethinking Innovation*,
https://doi.org/10.1007/978-3-031-40848-9_17

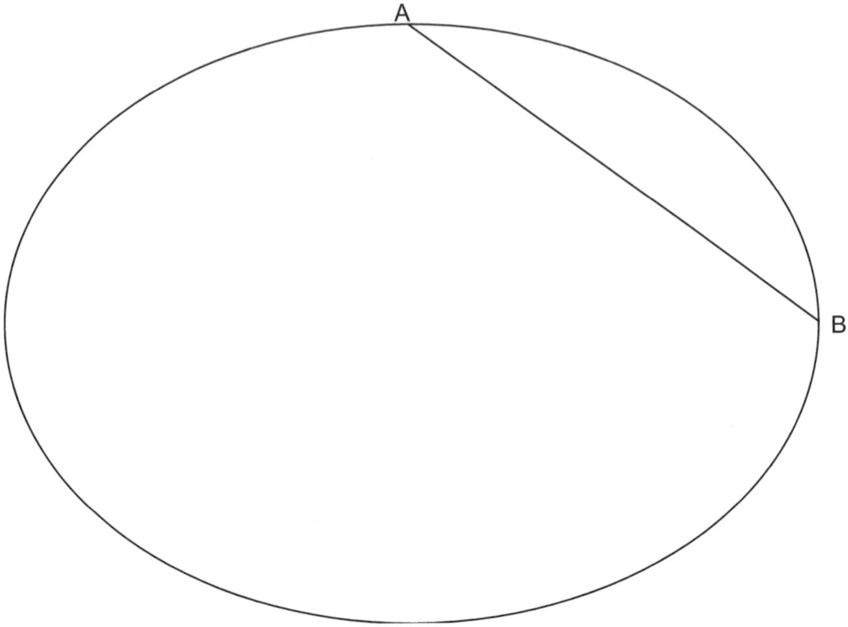

Fig. 17.1 When a circle becomes a straight line

of relationships that binds the relevant problem area together and gives meaning to the communication situation. Using a linear starting point when viewing the circle in Fig. 17.1 may easily end up with a situation, where one or more critical variables are designated as the cause and something else as its effect.

Most of us encounter problems when thinking in circular contexts, where several variables interact with each other. Instead, we reach for a simpler solution and view social phenomena that are circular as if they were linear. We set random boundaries so that of necessity we achieve the effect of following a linear path in relation to a cause we have selected. In this way, we punctuate the communication situation and establish 'model power' in relation to the other person(s). However, we often forget that it is only in the models of social reality where such linear relationships are represented, and that this does not reflect reality in the social sphere. We confuse the map for the terrain and operate as if the map is the terrain. If we do this, it may be obvious that the linear relationships are logically correct, but ultimately it is not the models that are interesting, but what they are supposed to represent and say something about: that is to say, the phenomenon / problem in the social sphere.

Examples of circular relationships are found throughout the social sphere: The working environment affects productivity, but productivity also affects the working environment. Aggressive behaviour leads to social rejection, which in turn reinforces aggressive behaviour. Parents raise their children, but children also 'raise' their parents. Teachers influence their students, but students also influence their

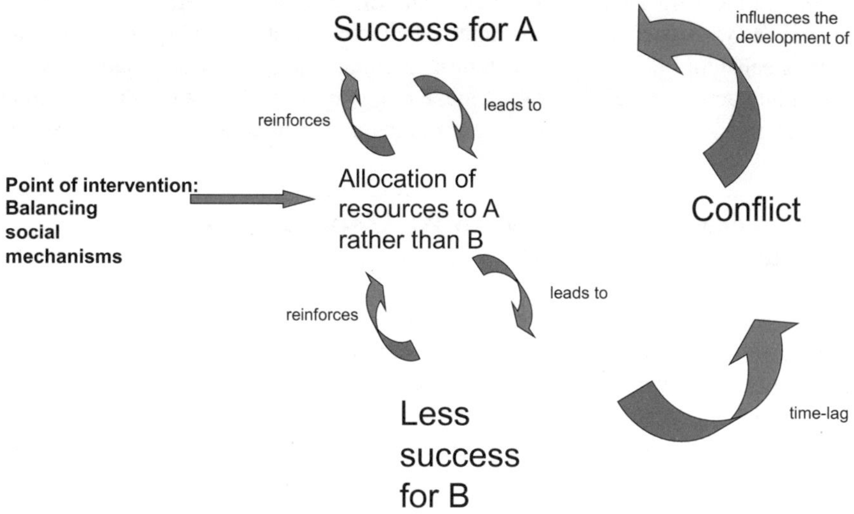

Fig. 17.2 Successful becomes more successful

teachers. The means influence the goal, but the goal also influences the means, and so on.

We have shown such a relationship in Fig. 17.2.

Breaking Patterns Creates Change

While the smallest unit of communication is a message, the unit of analysis is the pattern in which that message is included. A statement from one party leads to a reaction from the other, and in turn, this affects the first party. Simplified, we can say that a pattern in communication is formed by the sequence: statement, response and resultant. When several such actions and responses interact, processes arise where it is possible to uncover an underlying pattern. When several such processes are established, relationships between individuals and groups are formed. The individuals and groups then maintain and change the processes that they initially helped to form. The resultant is the part of the sequence that ensures that the utterance and the interpreter have an equal understanding of the message.

By means of their interactions, the group or several groups shape group norms and rules, which in turn help to maintain and/or change the group relations. The rules of social behaviour are thus created and transformed by individuals and/or groups of individuals, although there was no conscious intention to create them. The message always occurs in a cycle, where it is difficult to point to a beginning and an end. On the other hand, we can reveal the pattern in which the message is included.

In most cases, a change in social patterns can only be effected by changing one's own reactions to the other's behaviour, not by trying to change the other's behaviour directly. This is a principle that applies in most situations where social interactions take place over time, e.g. a marital conflict, a conflict within an organization, a conflict between organizations and even conflicts between nations.

Sociological Laws Arise When We Distinguish Between Intention and Behaviour

The extent to which the social sciences, and specifically the study of communication, have laws (scientific laws) depends on whether one has a restrictive or open interpretation of what a sociological law is. If we make a distinction in social science data between **intention and behaviour**, we can say that intention can be understood, while behaviour can be explained. In relation to behavioural explanations, sociological laws can be created, although these cannot explain everything that happens.

A pattern may be viewed as being made up of variables that are stable over a specific period of time. A sociological law is created by an observer who gains insight into a pattern.

By acquiring insight into a pattern of social behaviour, we may also have the possibility of predicting parts of the behaviour—at least in estimated terms within a short-term perspective. Sociological laws are further linked to specific societies in time and space. The connection to time and space also applies to physical laws, although these have a longer time perspective and are more general than sociological laws.

Exercises

1. Discuss the following statements:
   (a) A circle becomes a straight line when viewed on a very small scale.
   (b) Breaking patterns creates change.
2. As your starting point, take a situation at your workplace that often recurs, and answer the following questions:
   (a) Which elements are included?
   (b) How are the elements related to each other?
   (c) Can you recognize a pattern in the situation?
3. Choose a social incident in your local area.
   (a) List three points that you believe are the cause of the social incident and develop a model that shows a linear relationship.
   (b) What is the difference in understanding of the social incident if you first use a linear model and then a circular model?
4. Develop circular models, with positive and negative feedback loops, for the following situations:

(a) In a poor third-world country, the population increase has been very large in the last ten years. The river delta region has now become completely over-populated. A cyclone devastates the river delta region causing massive flooding, resulting in the deaths of 300,000 people.
(b) A single farmer settles on a fertile uninhabited plain. After forty years, much of the plain has been transformed into a city.
(c) A raindrop falls into a crack in the mountains. After fifty years, the mountain has become wooded.

5. Develop a circular model, with positive and negative feedback loops, showing the relationships between the following critical variables:

- The population of a city
- Industrialization
- Relocation
- Sanitary conditions
- The prevalence of illness
- Microbiota
- Waste.

6. Develop a circular model, with positive and negative feedback loops, showing the relationships between the following critical variables:

- Annoyance about a statement that has been made by somebody
- The number of people commenting on the statement
- The number of new ideas that emerge
- The fear of making a fool of oneself
- The quality of the proposed ideas
- Self-confidence
- People's understanding of what is being said
- The feeling of boredom.

7. Develop a circular model, with positive and negative feedback loops, showing the following critical variables:

- Pollution
- Population
- Technology
- Food supply
- Mortality rate
- Armed conflicts.

References

Abelson, R.P. (1981). The psychological status of the script concept. American Psychologist, 36: 715–721.

Ackoff, R.L. (1981). Creating the corporate future: Plan or be planned for, Wiley, London.

Adriaenssen, D.J. & Johannessen, J-A. (2016). Prospect theory as an explanation for resistance to organizational change: some management implications. Problems and Perspectives in Management, 14, 2: 84–92.

Aikins, de-Graft, A. (2011). Nonverbal communication in everyday multicultural life. In D. Hook, B. Franks & M.W. Bauer (eds.) The social psychology of communication, Palgrave, London. Pp. 67–87.

Anderson, J.R. (1990). Cognitive psychology and its implications, Freeman, New York.

Anderson, N.H. (1981). Foundations of information integration theory, Academic Press, New York.

Arden, D. (2015). Win-win, Pearson, New York

Arkes, H.R. & Blumer, C. (1985). The Psychology of sunk costs. Organizational Behaviour and Human Performance, 35: 129–140.

Axelrod, R. (1984). The evolution of cooperation, Basic Books, New York.

Bandler, R. (1993). Time for a change, Meta Publications Inc., New York.

Bandler, R. (1993a). The adventures of anybody, Meta Publications Inc., New York.

Bandler, R. & Grinder, J. (1975). The structure and magic, Science and Behaviour Books, New York.

Bandler, R. & Grinder, J. (1976). The structure and magic II, Science and Behaviour Books, New York.

Bandler, R. & Grinder, J. (1990). Frogs into Princes Eden Grove Editions, Middlesex

Bandler, R. & LaValle, J. (1996). Persuasion engineering, Meta Publications, New York.

Baron, R.A. (1990). Environmentally induced positive affect: Its impact on self-efficacy, task performance, negotiation, and conflict. Journal of Applied Social Psychology, 20: 368–384.

Bateson,G. (1972). Steps to an ecology of mind, Intex Books, London.

Bazerman, M.H. (1994). Judgement in managerial decision making, Wiley, New York.

Bazerman, M.H., Giuliano, T. & Appleman, A. (1984). Escalation in individual and group decision making. Organizational Behaviour and Human Performance, 33: 141–152.

Bazerman, M.H. & Lewicki, R.J. (ed.). (1983). Negotiating in Organizations, Sage, New York.

Bazerman, M.H., Mannix, E. & Thompson, L. (1988). Groups as mixed-motive negotiations. In I.E.J. Lawler & B. Markovsky (ed.), Advances in group processes: Theory and Research, Vol. 5, JAI Press, Greenwich, Conn.

Bendor, J., Kramer, R.M. & Stout, S. (1991). When in doubt: Cooperation in the noisy prisoners dilemma. Journal of Conflict Resolution, 35: 691–719.

Bowers, J.W., Metts, S.M. & Duncanson, W.T. (1985). Emotion and interpersonal communication. In M.L. Knapp & G.R. Miller (eds.), Handbook of Interpersonal communication, Sage, London. Pp. 500–550.

Bouty, I & Drucker-Godard, C. (2018). Managerial work and coordination: A practice-based approach on board a racing sailboat. Human Relations, 72, 3: 565–587.

Bunge, M. (1996). Finding philosophy in social science, New Haven CT: Yale University Press

Bunge, M. (1997). Mechanism and explanation. Philosophy of the Social Sciences 27: 410–465.

Bunge, M. (1998). Social science under debate, University of Toronto Press, Toronto.

Bunge, M. (1999). The sociology-philosophy connection, Transaction Publishers, New Brunswick, NJ.

Carnevale, P.J. & Conlon, D. (1987). Time pressure and mediator strategy in simulated organizational dispute. Organizational behaviour and Human Decision Processes, 40: 111–133.

Cialdini, R.B. (1993). Influence: Science and practice, HarperCollins, New York.

Csikszentmihalyi, M. (2013). Creativity: The psychology of discovery and invention, Harper, New York.

Dermer, M. & Thiel, D.L. (1975). When beauty may fail. Journal of Personality and Social Psychology, 31: 1168–1176.

Dion, K., Berscheid, E. & Hatfield, E. (1972). What is beautiful is good. Journal of Personality and Social Psychology, 24: 285–290.

Dixit, A.K. & Nalebuff, D.J. (2010). The art of strategy, W.W. Norton, New York.

Dowell, N.M.M., Nixon, T.M. & Graesser, A.C. (2018). Group communication analysis. Behaviour Research Methods, 51, 3: 1007–1041.

Foster, W.M., Hassard, J.S., Morris, J. & Wolfram, J. (2019). The changing nature of managerial work: The effects of corporate restructuring on management jobs and careers. Human Relations, 72, 3:473–504.

Holm Pedersen, L., Hjelmar, U. & Bhatti, Y. (2018). What does the minister do? On the working conditions of political leaders. Public Administration, 96, 2: 259–275.

Holmes. W.T. & Parker, M.A. (2016). Communication. International Journal of Business Communication, 54, 1: 70–82.

Janis, I.L. (1982). Group think, Houghton Muffins, New York.

Johannessen, J-A. (2018). Innovation leads to economic crises, Palgrave, London.

Johannessen, J-A. (2020). The workplace of the future, Routledge, London.

Johannessen, J-A. (2020a). Automation, innovation and economic crises: Survival the fourth industrial revolution, Routledge, London.

Johannessen, J-A. (2020b). Artificial intelligence, automation and the future of competence at work, Routledge.

Johannessen, J-A. (2020c). Knowledge management for leadership and communication: AI, innovation and the digital economy, Emerald, London.

Johannessen, J-A. (2020d). Knowledge management philosophy: Communication as a strategic asset in knowledge management, Emerald, London.

Johannessen, J-A. (2021). China's innovation economy: Artificial intelligence and the new silk road, Routledge, London.

Johannessen, J-A. (2021a). Artificial intelligence, automation and ethics in the innovation economy, Routledge, London.

Johannessen, J-A. (2021b). Communication as social theory: The social side of knowledge management, Emerald, London.

Johannessen, J-A. (2022). Creativity, innovation and the fourth industrial revolution: The da Vinci strategy, Routledge, London.

Johannessen, J-A. (2022a). The new silk road and the innovation economy in China, Routledge, London.

Johannessen, J-A. (2022b). The philosophy of tacit knowledge, Emerald, London.

Johannessen, J-A. (2022c). A systemic approach to continuous change in the innovation economy, Routledge, London.

Johannessen, J-A. (2022d). Intelligent robots consciousness and creativity: The search for hidden knowledge, the cognitive side of knowledge management, Emerald, London.

Johannessen, J-A. (2023). A Marxist interpretation of Church leadership: Romans: 13: 1–7. Lexington Books, New York.

Johannessen, J-A. (2023a). Feudal capitalism: The political economy of the innovation society, Routledge, London.

Johannessen, J-A. (2023b). De-globalization, China-US tensions in the Innovation Economy, Routledge, London.

Johannessen, J-A. (2023c). Artificial intelligence and creativity: Implications for automation in the innovation economy, Routledge, London.

Johannessen, J-A. (2023d). The fourth industrial revolution and the labor market: Future proofing work in the innovation economy, Routledge, London.

Johannessen, J-A. (2023e). Aspects of a theory of genocide, Trivent Publishong, London.

Kidron, A. & Vinarski-Peretz, H. (2018). The political iceberg: the hidden side of leaders' political behaviour. Leadership & Organization Development Journal, 39, 8:1010–1023.

Lakoff, G. & Johnson, M. (2003). Metaphors we live by, University of Chicago Press, Chicago.

Luhmann, N. (1996). Social systems, Stanford University Press, Stanford.

Lundqvist, D., Eriksson, F. & Ekberg, K. (2018). Managers' social support: Facilitators and hindrances for seeking support at work. Work, 59, 3: 351–365.

Matsuo, M. (2017). The unlearning of managerial skills: A qualitative study of executive officers. European Management Review, 16, 2: 303–315.

Milgram, S. (2010). Obedience to authority, Pinter & Martin, London.

Miller, J.G. (1978). Living systems, McGraw-Hill, New York.

Mintzberg, H. (2013). Simply managing: What managers do-and can do better, FT Publishing, New York.

Nisbett, R.E. & Ross, L. (1980). Human inference: Strategies and shortcomings of social judgement, Prentice Hall, Englewood Cliffs, NJ.

Peticca-Harris, A. (2018). Managing compassionately? Managerial narratives about grief and compassion. Human Relations, 72, 3: 588–612.

Polanyi, M. (1958). Personal knowledge, Routledge & Kegan Paul, London.

Pruitt, D.G. & Rubin, J.Z. (1986).. Social conflict: Escalation, stalemate and settlement, McGraw Hill, New York.

Pruitt, D.G. & Syna, H. (1985). Mismatching the opponents offers in negotiation. Journal of experimental Social Psychology, 21: 103–113.

Putnam, L.L. (1985). Bargaining as organizational communication. In R.D. McPhee & P.K. Tomkins (ed.), Organizational communication: Traditional themes and new directions. Vol. 13, Sage, New York.

Schøn, D. (1983). The reflective practitioner. How professionals think in action, Basic Books, New York.

Schøn, D. (1987). Educating the reflective practitioner, Jossey-Bass, London

Schwab, K. (2017). The fourth industrial revolution, Portfolio Penguin, New York.

Slovic, P. & Lichtenstein, S. (1971). Comparison of Bayesian and regression approaches in the study of information processing in judgement. Organizational Behaviour and Human Performance, 6: 649–744.

Smith, D. (2005). Institutional ethnography. A sociology for people, AltaMira Press, New York.

Smorczewska, B. (2018). Leadership as the construction of one's own story. Australian Journal of Career Development, 27, 2: 81–87.

Strugar-Jelača, M. (2018). Redefining the management roles: Response to digital networking and access to a large amount of information. Strategic Management, 23, 2: 42–49.

Tengblad, S. (2006). Is there a new managerial work? A comparison with Henry Mintzberg's study 30 years later. Journal of managerial Studies, 43, 7: 1437–1461.

Thompson, L.L. (1990). An examination of naive and experienced negotiators. Journal of Personality and Social Psychology, 59: 82–90.

Thompson, L.L. (1991a). Information exchange in negotiation. Journal of experimental Social Psychology, 27: 161–179.

Tversky, A. & Kahneman, D. (2000). Loss aversion in riskless choice. In D. Kahneman, & A. Tversky (eds.), Choices, values and frames, Cambridge University Press, Cambridge. Pp. 143–158.

Van Quaquebeke, N. & Will Felps, W. (2018). Respectful inquiry: A motivational account of leading through asking questions and listening. Academy of Management Review, 43, 1: 5–27.

Vis, B. (2010). Politics of risk-taking, Amsterdam University, Amsterdam.

Watzlawick, P. (1993). The situation is hopeless, but not serious, W.W. Norton, New York.

Watzlawick, P. (2014). Pragmatics of human communication, W.W. Norton, New York.

Weick, K.E. (1979). The social psychology of organizing, McGraw-Hill, New York.

Zubek, J.M., Pruitt, D.G., Peirce, R.S., McGillicaddy, N.B. & Syna, H. (1992). Short term success in mediation: Its relationship to disputant and mediator behaviours and prior conditions. Journal of Conflict Resolution, 36: 546–572.

Part II

Personal Communication Tools

Personal Strategies

18

Aims in this Chapter

1. Too reflect on self-management
2. In this chapter, the reader should reflect on the following concepts: personal change competence, personal achievements, personal benchmarking, personal motivation strategy, personal mastery skills and personal reputation.

Tools for Communication

Personal strategies in communication and the personal communication tools we develop in Part II are an attempt to promote the individual's communication skills. There are four elements in personal communication, as understood here, that promote interaction between people to promote the system's results. These four elements are:

- Self-awareness is linked to the business's results.
- An action plan is prepared.
- What is to be achieved for the individual is based on the company's needs.
- The tools are structured and for improving the individual's communication skills.

We have had these four elements as a backdrop when we have developed part II.

The formal communication process is based on three sizes, which mutually support each other:

K. Ledingham et al., *Rethinking Innovation*,
https://doi.org/10.1007/978-3-031-40848-9_18

- Relationship
- Process
- Results.

Communication theory is not a specific theory, but many theories. The communication theory we use as a starting point for developing the personal communication tools is based on systemic thinking.

In the communication process, there are many techniques that can be used. The development of a focus on communication tools began in earnest in the late 1980s and has only increased in strength. One explanation for the widespread use of such tools may be the increasing complexity that managers experience as a result of increased change and turbulence, as well as the increasing competition in the global knowledge economy. Another explanation for the widespread use of communication in the management process may be the emphasis on companies' intangible resources to promote results at all levels in companies.

Communication and coaching are closely related variables. The biggest difference between communication and coaching is that in coaching you must achieve clearly defined goals and promote performance. Coaching is understood in this way as a tool for the leader. It is this understanding that we base ourselves on when developing the personal communication tools in Part II.

With such an understanding, the history of coaching is as old as communication. However, it is coaching from the sports world and sports psychology that was adopted as a model for the coaching movement from the 1960s. However, coaching has only been used in private and public companies since the 1990s as a special method of management. This can be explained by the strong emphasis that organizational learning received in the 1990s. Linking coaching to the development of the learning organization is considered important, because coaching as a tool promotes behavioural change, which is considered important for developing the learning organization.

The leader as a coach includes both individual coaching and team coaching. In both types of coaching, it is more about asking the right questions than coming up with the right answers and solutions. An important purpose of coaching is to get the other person or others to reflect on the questions and come up with the answers that they believe will promote their performance. Another purpose of coaching is to promote change in the individual, the team and the social system of which they are a part. In this way, coaching can be understood as a social mechanism for promoting change. Coaching can in this way be used as a tool to develop a new future for the organization.

The purpose of the personal communication tools developed in Part II is to bring out and develop the potential of the individual and the team. To achieve this, it is important to develop the 'eye for the future' in the individual and the team. This means creating an understanding of urgency, a proactive future-oriented attitude.

There are three basic values in the personal communication tools developed in Part II. These values are:

- Always show **respect** for the other person or persons.
- Take **responsibility** for the other person's or others' experience of the situation.
- Always have the **dignity** of the other or others as a backdrop.

Self-Management

In the emerging knowledge economy, service and knowledge workers must increasingly take care of their own career development, because companies will have enough to compete in the global knowledge economy. It is through knowing one's own strengths and weaknesses, opportunities and obstacles that the individual can develop their personal change competence, their personal achievements, be able to benchmark themselves against the best, develop their personal motivation strategy, their personal coping skills and their personal reputation. It is these six dimensions we work with in this section that we choose to call self-management. We have shown the relationship between the quantities we work with to develop self-management in Fig. 18.1.

He who manages to lead himself will be the winner in the knowledge economy, says Drucker (2005: 100). Most people know a little about their weaknesses, but to a lesser extent their strengths, and one can develop their achievements by gaining greater insight into one's weaknesses (see Drucker 2005: 100). It is only when the window of opportunity is so large and the choices so many, as is the case in the global knowledge economy, that there is a real need to develop insight into what one is good at, and then develop these aspects of oneself. In earlier times when the

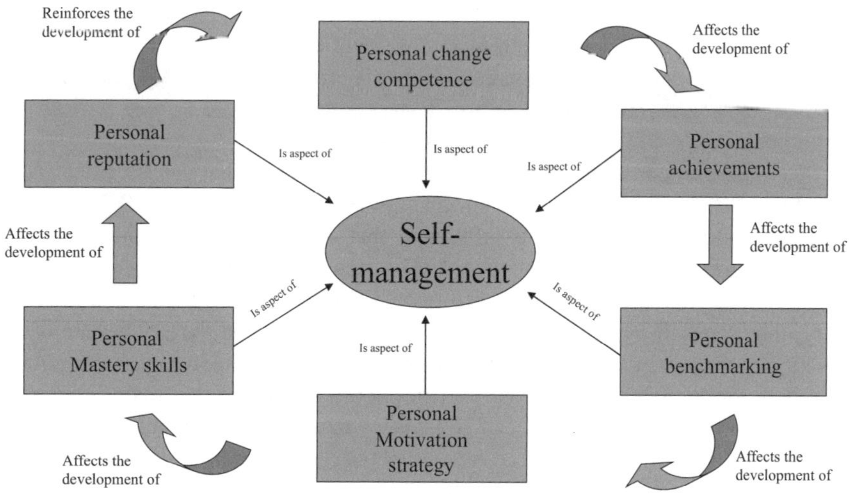

Fig. 18.1 Self-management: six elements

stability of the outside world was relatively great, and the rate of change was relatively small, the need for continuous development of the individual strengths was of less importance than in today's global knowledge economy where the rate of change is great and the complexity is great. It is this shift in perspective that makes self-management an important challenge for the individual. Self-management is based on interaction skills and emotional intelligence. In practice, this means that all aspects of feedback are central to self-management. One aspect of feedback that is little noticed is the type of feedback referred to as feedforward. This is a mechanism of expectation, which each of us builds into our actions. Our expectations influence our behaviour here and now. It is therefore important that we make explicit for ourselves the expectations we have for a situation. By making expectations explicit, we have opportunities to learn from the results and thus improve our performance. All six elements of Fig. 18.1 are somehow connected to different types of feedback. Feedback is the most central element in interaction skills and emotional intelligence. In this way, there is a close connection between interaction skills, emotional intelligence and self-management.

Self-management is understood as feedback analysis (see Drucker 2005) a simple concept for winning in the knowledge economy. In the rest of this chapter, we go into each of the quantities in fig. x. We unfold both a greater degree of complexity in the concepts and also an opportunity to develop strength in areas we did not know before. It is these areas of oneself that are the most difficult to work with, because they are often unknown to us, even though they are probably known to others. It is this constant interaction between feedback analysis and the development of strengths we are not aware of, that makes self-management an important part of the individual's personal development in the knowledge society. When you work with the exercises and the practical coaching tools in self-management, the personal improvements will not show immediately. Drucker (2005: 102) says that if you work consistently with fatback analysis, it will take two to three years before you gain insight into your own strength. We are of the opinion that a similar period of time will apply to self-management. This may mean that the book should be set up as a book you continuously return to over a two- to three = year period, and not a book you read from cover to cover in a short time.

Self-management is the transition from the question: What should I do? to the question: What should my contribution be? (see Drucker 2005: 106). The last question is linked to making a difference that really matters to oneself and to others. To cope with this, you have to develop aspects of yourself that you may not even know if you have the potential to make a difference. To do this, one must not only know oneself, one must actively take responsibility in the relationships one enters into, or should enter into, in order to become acquainted with the strengths of others. In this way, one can together develop a difference that really matters.

A not insignificant side effect of self-management is that you get a tool to deal with your superiors, as well as your colleagues and subordinates. A banal but important insight is that if you are to lead your superiors, colleagues and subordinates, then you should familiarize yourself with their goals and the demands and challenges that they feel are present.

Finding out what really matters to the other, superior, colleague or subordinate, is the crucial point in leading others. This is also a key point in self-management, i.e. defining the goals and challenges that one should commit to, and thus also those that one should opt out of.

What we have written so far in this introduction is, that it will be a waste of time to try to repair areas you are not good at. You have the most to gain from developing the areas and abilities you are already good at. Feedback is often given in areas where improvements are needed, and to a lesser extent in areas you are already good at before. This comes also expressed in the fact that one is more prepared to deal with criticism than praise. When developing your own feedback analysis, you should therefore also directly ask for feedback in the areas you are good at, precisely in order to be able to develop these to perfection. One should therefore choose one's respondents carefully and be part of a network that has the development of mutual forces as a stated goal.

Self-management is as Fig. 18.1 also shows connected to develop their personal reputation. For this, we need to develop a personal story about ourselves, which others will get involved in. In order for someone to get involved in your personal story, you must build the classic elements into a story. These elements are scroll described by Ibarra and Lineback (2005: 64–74).

The main elements of a classic story are connected to the fact that something has changed, i.e. you first present the feature that will arouse immediate interest. You must then bring out the drama, such as tensions and conflicts that this brought to you. Then, you show how this ended in success or tragedy. This will grab the others and make it easier for you to promote the personal reputation that you want to convey.

Be aware of the message so far: If you try to improve in the areas you are not good at, then you will have difficulty performing at the top where you have the best conditions to become really good, because it requires time, energy and many types of resources to improve in all areas. Then, there will necessarily be less energy and commitment left to develop where you already have the prerequisites to be among the best.

The underlying variables in self-management, as we have emphasized them in this introduction, are the following:

- Feedback analysis
- To understand the goals and challenges of others
- To focus on what you are good at
- To be part of a network that is committed to developing mutual strength in what you are already good at
- To develop a personal story.

In the following, we will consider each element in Fig. 18.1

Reference

Drucker, P.F. (2005). Managing yourself, Harvard Business Review, Jan, I Harvard Business School, On Print Collection, produkt nr. 8762, s. 3–16.

Communication and Personal Change Skills

19

Aims of this Chapter

1. There are two purposes in this chapter. The first is to break out of habits that have a limiting effect on one's own ability to change. Secondly, it is to understand how the cleaning affects the behaviour.
2. In this chapter, the reader should reflect on the following concepts: feedback and flexibility as a basis for change, intention and communication as a basis for change and behavioural patterns as a basis for change.

Feedback and Flexibility as a Basis for Change

Ask yourself the following questions: How many of the relationships you are in, would it be an advantage if you had handled the feedback in a more appropriate way?

The universal feedback model is called TUTE, i.e. test, perform, test, effects. The model briefly states that we must know what we want to achieve. Secondly, we do this with a great deal of flexibility. Then, the operation is tested. When we are satisfied with the test, we effect this and set ourselves new goals.

This univocal feedback model depends on three factors:

1. How we give feedback.
2. How we receive feedback.
3. How the feedback is integrated into our behaviour.

K. Ledingham et al., *Rethinking Innovation*,
https://doi.org/10.1007/978-3-031-40848-9_19

To Give Feedback

The purpose of our feedback is very important. If you are slightly annoyed when the feedback is given, it is unlikely that the other will get the full benefit of your feedback. The intention of the feedback must be benign and you must be perceived as engaged. If the feedback is to be useful, it must be able to help improve performance. The feedback should therefore always contain a message that seems encouraging and a section that contains specific information on what needs to be improved. As a general rule, feedback should not be formulated as criticism. If there is criticism you want to give, then you should focus on the positive and on the potential that lies in the opportunities for improvement.

To Receive Feedback

There are two main ways to receive feedback:

- As a critique
- As an aid

Framing a feedback that criticism helps to hinder learning and change. If you frame a feedback as an aid, there will be a potential for improvement. The attitude one should have when receiving a feedback is that one is grateful for the feedback and seems curious about how the other can help one to improve the feedback.

Feedback understood in this perspective is only interesting if you can make changes as a consequence of them.

Integrating Feedback into Behaviour

Being receptive to feedback is a prerequisite for learning. If we do not try to change the behaviour as a consequence of the feedback, it has no effect.

Most of our behaviours are automated habits and habits, such as our phrases, our daily routines, our rituals and our attitudes. The key to integrating new behaviours is to learn old behaviours. This can be done by improving, planning and rehearsing.

The best way to change the behaviour of others is to change your own reaction to the behaviour of others. This presupposes that we can exercise a great deal of flexibility in relation to our own reactions to the behaviour of others.

It is only by building in sufficient variation in one's own pattern of action that one can influence the behaviour of others. This is called the Flexibility Act or Ashby's (1956) Act on Sufficient Variation. A person who uses this law as a starting point for his own actions constantly thinks about how he should change in relation to the other's behaviour. He does not necessarily do this to adapt to the other, but because he knows that this is the best way to influence their behaviour.

His main question will always be: How can I change to promote change in one or the other?

The greater the complexity of the world around us, the more flexibility is required to achieve one's own goals. Therefore, variety should be built in as an important part of the personal ability to change. Having all the eggs in one basket will not be an appropriate strategy when the rate of change, turbulence and complexity in the outside world are high.

Flexibility or variety is a prerequisite for tackling diversity. The greater the degree of variation you can bet on, the greater the likelihood of success, when the complexity is great. Therefore, the millipede's strategy, the fact that you have a diversity to play on, is an appropriate strategy in a turbulent world.

For each action that a person chooses, you must be able to respond with the same reaction plus an extra variation. This is called flexible response and has been used at many different system levels throughout history. If you do not have this extra variety to play on, you will quickly get caught up in the other person's behaviour. On the personal level, flexible response is a strategy for influencing and controlling one's own surroundings.

When the complexity of the world around you increases, you can relate to it in two ways. One can reduce the complexity if possible. One can absorb the complexity by increasing the flexibility.

Intention and Communication as a Basis for Change

Intention is usually understood as the purpose or goal of our behaviour. Intention can also be understood as what we seek to achieve with our behaviour. Whether we manage to achieve our intentions is, among other things, depending on the personal resources we are able to mobilize.

It is often the case that problems arise because we misinterpret intention and behaviour. We can easily refer to behaviours, for example as threatening, aggressive or the like. When we interpret the behaviour as aggressive, we often respond accordingly.

What we do less often, however, is look for the intention behind a behaviour. This has its explanation in that behaviour is more visible, while the intention is more hidden from us. One technique or attitude that can be helpful is to look at all intention as positive, and then interpret the behaviour based on this assumption.

When we make this distinction between intention and behaviour at the same time as we incorporate the assumption that all intention is positive on one level or another, we increase our own possibilities for dealing with situations. This increases our flexibility, frees up our resources for communication, and that we influence our own and others' behaviour patterns.

When we are faced with a behaviour we do not understand, the technique is to work with ourselves, to intervene with the positive intention behind the behaviour. The positive intention behind what we experience as aggressive behaviour may be a desire to protect oneself or one's family. It can also be a strong commitment to something that we interpret as aggressive behaviour. The positive intention behind fear and anxiety may be the search for security. The positive intention behind anger may be the desire to maintain boundaries, one's own dignity and identity.

It can often be enlightening to search for deeper intentions to find the positive intention behind any behaviour. This gives us more room for manoeuvre which increases the diversity of variation.

When we communicate a message to someone, the first thing we do is translate our thoughts and feelings into a language. The next step is to choose the medium, to reach the other. The recipient then interprets the message and responds in one way or another. This is a complicated system, which often breaks down. Confusion and misinterpretation occur on a large scale. A simple course of action to reduce complexity is as follows: When you receive feedback that you find inappropriate, try to go behind the response and find the positive intention. The meaning of communication is as a general rule in the message you receive, so it is an important point how you interpret this message.

We do not respond with any necessity to what is said, but to how we interpret what is said. Each person has their own mental model of the world. The more we know about the other person's mental model, the better we will be able to communicate with that person. The richer and more diverse your own mental model of the world is, the easier it will be to communicate with others.

In order for the communication not to break down, feedback is crucial. This is where it is important to make an artifice between intention and behaviour, and always to interpret the intention positively, no matter how difficult it may seem from the behaviour. It can be said so strongly that there is feedback that can promote any inhibition of communication. Therefore, make it a rule in any communication to look for positive intentions behind any feedback.

In communication, there are four basic elements. These are people, message, media and result. Communication can be described as follows: Someone (persons) has talked to someone (persons) about something (message), over certain channels (media) with a certain effect (result). In any communication strategy, there are four questions that should be considered:

- People: What is the prevailing mental model or models?
- Message: What is the actual message?
- Media: How should the message be wrapped?
- Result: What is the desired effect?

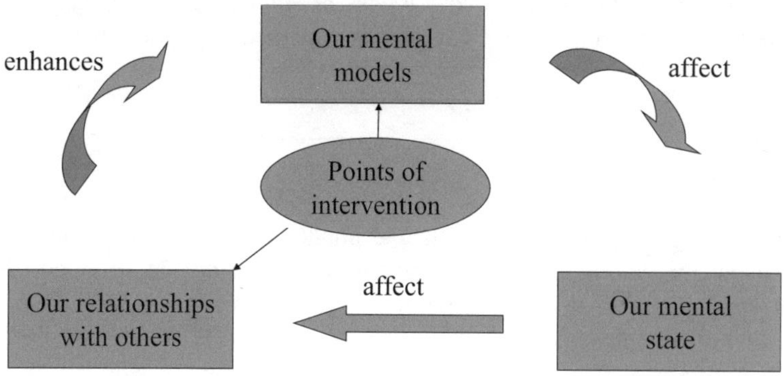

Fig. 19.1 Maintaining our mental models

Behaviour Pattern as a Basis for Change

We are largely social addicts. Some habits lead us to achieve results, while other habits lead us to use our resources in a less favourable way. It is our mental models, developed over time, that affect our mental state to a great extent, and which in turn affect our relationships with others. The relationships we enter into usually reinforce our mental models (Fig. 19.1).

Our Mental Models

Respect is a prerequisite for good communication. One does not have to agree with the other to show respect. One shows respect by understanding and accepting the other's mental model of reality. The point is, no one has the right map of reality. Different maps or mental models cover different aspects of reality. The perspective we take will always be relative to the position one takes or has. To understand this statement, try the following experiment. Stand on a chair and draw a horizontal circle in the air. You should draw the circle with your index finger the way the sun goes. While drawing the circle in the air in the way described, ask a person to sit down below you and look up at the circle you are drawing. Ask the person to say which direction you are drawing, with or against the sun. The result may seem surprising, but only says that the perspective we take is relative to the position we are in.

Our mental models develop over time by using our senses when we select something and thus away something else, when we generalize and when we focus on some of what we have chosen and thus tone down something else. In this way, we structure our personal experiences. How we structure our personal experiences says something about the pattern that shapes our mental models, controls our thinking and influences our behaviour.

We can use our ideas to colour, emphasize something and enhance parts of the experiences. In this way, we can change our mental patterns that govern our behaviour.

Our Mental State

You can have great knowledge, skills and qualifications. This does not help you much if your mental state does not support what you are going to do. When a top athlete prepares for a competition, he spends a lot of time building himself up mentally, not just physically. Building the mental state is an integral part of his training programme. The same principle also applies to those who are to perform a lot in other arenas.

For example, a leader can create a visionary situation, a surgeon can create a state of focused operation, a chess player can create a state of tactical genius, an artist a creative state, a teacher a committed and participatory state, etc. The question for you is the following: What mental state would change your performance so that you performed at the top in the area you work with? Are there any of the following states that would have been helpful to you: focused, analytical, creative, associative, persuasive, calm, energetic, etc.? Can you imagine any situations where any of these conditions would be of help to you? Describe one of these situations and develop a condition that would have been helpful in performing optimally in this situation.

Our Relationships with Others

Our relationships with others can be understood on different logical levels:

- Purpose: What do we seek to achieve with our behaviour?
- Identity: What role do I have?
- Values: What is important to me?
- Competence: What knowledge, skills and attitude do I have towards what I am going to do?
- Behaviour: What am I doing?

It is easier to adjust and possibly change at a lower logical level, such as behaviour, than at a higher logical level, such as values. The assumption we build on here is that the higher logical levels affect the lower logical levels, and all levels are expressed through the behaviour shown. This indicates that the changes will be more radical if they are made at a higher logical level. When change is required, this model can be used in a coherent way to be able to make the right interventions.

Exercises

Feedback and flexibility as a basis for change

1. Imagine a real situation in your workplace or home situation, where you have given another person feedback on something he has done.
   a. What was your intention?
   b. How was the feedback perceived?
   c. How would you like the other person's behaviour to change?
2. Now imagine a real situation in your workplace or home situation where someone gives you feedback.
   a. Did you perceive the feedback as a hidden criticism?
   b. Did you perceive the feedback as a genuine opportunity to learn something new?
   c. What did you learn?
   d. Did what you learned change any of your behaviour?
3. Imagine a communication situation at work or at home where you felt that you were locked (inflexible). Reflect on three alternative strategies that could have led to you becoming more flexible, and thus gaining greater control over the situation.
4. In the next communication situation you are in, already think through three different communication strategies, which will make you achieve greater flexibility. Then practice on these as soon as you have an opportunity.

Intention and communication

5. Imagine a situation where you were really annoyed by someone else's behaviour. Try to find the positive intention behind the behaviour.
6. Think of a situation where you noticed that the other person or people did not like or understand your behaviour. Examine your own intentions behind the behaviour.
7. Imagine a communication situation in a work context or in the home situation that has made a big impression on you, positively or negatively.
   a. Examine now
      i. your own intentions
      ii. what you think was the other person's intentions
      iii. how you interpreted the other person's intention
      iv. how you think the other person interpreted your intentions
      v. your mental model in the situation
      vi. what you think was the other person's mental model in the situation
      vii. the very message of communication
      viii. whether the relationship you have or had with the other person influenced your interpretation
      ix. whether the selected channel was adequate

x. if you had clarified what you would achieve with the communication
xi. about the context put some restrictions on communication
xii. whether there were any unwritten rules that were leading.

8. Based on this study, how would you have changed your own communication strategy in this situation? Will such a changed communication strategy be helpful in later communication situations? List the lessons you can learn from this study, which can help you improve your own communication in the future.

Behaviour pattern as a basis for change

9. Think of any experience that has made a very strong impression on you, and where it did not go the way you thought it would. Imagine this experience as a movie in your inner theatre. Run this movie in your inner theatre for five minutes. Then describe the event in the film as a story with a beginning, a middle part and an end. Now play the movie again. Now you are deliberately colouring some objects or events in the movie. Add sound and emotion to the objects or events you selected. Now turn 180 degrees in space and change some other objects or events in the movie. Colour them, add sound to them and give them emotions. Now reduce both of these objects or events so that they mean less in the movie. Do this something with the whole movie. Now enlarge these objects or events so that they dominate in the movie. Does this change any of the whole of the film? What you have done is examine some of your automatic reflexes, habits and habits.
10. Try to remember the last communication you entered into. How many times did you fill in information that the other person did not convey? How many times did you speak before the other person finished speaking? Think about it, this is important, because you probably interpreted a lot of what the other person said on the basis of the information you filled in yourself. How often did you notice that there were misinterpretations or slight irritation in this communication? Could this have something to do with you filling in the information yourself?
11. How often have you passed on to others this type of information, which you have filled in yourself? Never, then you should think again.
12. Think through the last week. If you could have changed some of your behaviour, what would you have changed? How would you have changed that? What would you seek to achieve by changing your behaviour?
13. Think about a relationship conflict you have had in your workplace or home situation. Try to interpret the conflict from the following logical levels:
    a. Purpose
    b. Role
    c. Values
    d. Competence
    e. Behaviour.

Personal Communication Coaching Tools: Perspective Analysis

Explanation of perspective analysis

What is perspective analysis? It is the interpretation of the experiences that depends on the position from which the experiences are perceived. There are three different perspectives that have proven to be useful in practice:

- You see the situation from your own point of view.
- You see the situation from the point of view of the other or the others.
- You take the perspective of an observer who cares.

Different perspectives

What does it mean to have different perspectives? It means gaining a greater understanding of a situation, access to more information, greater ability to change and to get out of fixed behaviour patterns. Perspective analysis is absolutely crucial for personal change. You can also gain insight into how your behaviour affects others by practising perspective analysis. The perspective analysis helps you to see a situation from different angles. This gives you more leeway to make the necessary changes.

Examining one's own desires and feelings is the first perspective. Examining the desires and feelings of others is another perspective. Seeing oneself through the eyes of an observer is the third perspective.

Perspective analysis can be used in many contexts. When you experience a conflict in a relationship and feel locked in, perspective analysis can help you mobilize greater personal change ability. Perspective analysis can also be helpful in any impact assessment you carry out, because it adds variation to the evaluations.

Exercise

Imagine a communication conflict that you have experienced, and that went into you, and that created a conflict between you and another. If you look at the situation from the first perspective (own point of view), how would you evaluate the conflict? Write down some key words.

If you look at the situation from a different perspective, how would you evaluate the conflict? Write down some key words.

If you look at the conflict from a third perspective, a neutral observer who cares, how would you evaluate the conflict? Write down some key words.

Now look at the key words you have written down. How can you use the differences that have certainly emerged? Is it possible for you to change something in your own perspective?

List three points that you can change with yourself to avoid similar conflicts in the future. Now think about how you want to proceed to change in relation to the three points you have listed.

Reference

Ashby, W.R. (1956). Introduction to cybernetics, Chapman & hall, London.

Communication and Personal Achievements 20

Aims of this Chapter

1. To understand how to set goals in a communication process
2. In this chapter, the reader should reflect on the following concepts: historical reason, goal orientation, core values and top performance.

Assumptions

The assumption we build on here is that in order to perform to the maximum, this presupposes a clear goal orientation, i.e. we must know what we want, why we want to achieve the goal, how we want to achieve the goal, and what we seek to achieve with the goal achievement.

Why we want to achieve the goal is here understood as a historical reason. What we seek to achieve with the goal is here linked to an expectation mechanism, i.e. a future situation. There are ten factors we should reflect on if we want to achieve the goals we set ourselves. We have grouped each of these factors under each of the four quantities in Fig. 20.1.

Linking personal achievement to our core values

We attract in a strange way success when our goals and our vision are linked to our core values. When the goal is linked to the vision, each role we have will give us the opportunity to express the basic values, at the same time as it creates meaning here and now. Clear bold goals that are supported by and support under the vision give energy to the actions we must take to approach the goal. The following assumes that you set aside time to develop your own personal vision.

We can divide our roles into four main groups. The roles in these groups overlap and influence each other. The four main groups of roles are as follows:

K. Ledingham et al., *Rethinking Innovation*,
https://doi.org/10.1007/978-3-031-40848-9_20

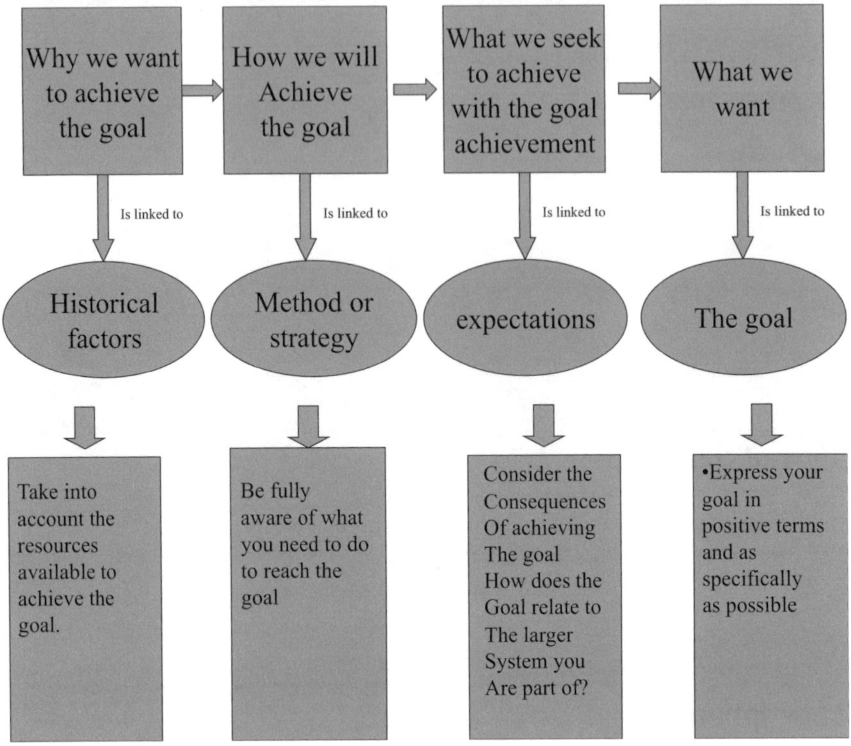

Fig. 20.1 Goal orientation and critical factors

- The work role: This consists of service to others at your workplace.
- The role of society: This consists of service to the local community, society and nature.
- The role of life: It consists of your own service to yourself.
- Personal role: This consists of service to family and friends.

The assumption here is that your life role forms the basis for the other three main types of roles. Your life role can be, for example, artist, athlete, educator, leader, etc. Your life role is reflected in your inner communication with yourself. How kindly do you address yourself? Do you address yourself in positive terms? What are you addressing as? It's what you identify with, which is your life's role. In the mirror you see a person. This is the person you need to make your best friend. The question is what you need to do to make this happen. We very rarely think about the relationship to ourselves. In order to promote personal achievement, it is crucial that we intervene in the relationship with ourselves. Your relationship with yourself can be improved in a very simple way. In short, you start by talking positively about yourself.

Work roles are increasingly shifting towards life roles in modern society. Work roles can be coach, lawyer, secretary, doctor, etc. However, work roles change more than the life role. What is your current job role? List your previous work roles. How many of them are equal to your current job role? How many are equal to what you identify as the role of your life? Do you like your current job role? Is the work role in line with your vision and your core values? If you do not like your work role, and it goes against your personal vision and your basic values, you should think about changing work role. If you cannot do this concretely by changing work role, then you can do the following. The first thing you do is change your work role mentally. This means that you frame it in a new way. Then you start thinking about it in a more positive way. Finally, you try to change the work role or parts of its content.

Good relationships with others seem to be what matter most to personal satisfaction. Your personal role is connected to the people who mean the most to you in your life. The acid test here is the following question: If your life depended on someone donating a kidney to you, who would you think stood up for you? The answer to this question is also the people you are going to provide the greatest service to now, not because they want to help you in a crisis situation, but because they are the people who mean the most to you in your life.

In the role of society, you must show a service attitude towards your local environment and nature, i.e. the larger system you are part of. The point here is that you can make a difference so that the local environment changes for the better. There will always be individuals or small groups of people who inspire change, so what the individual does is not insignificant.

With this review and the exercises that are linked to this review, you have now developed and improved your vision. Go through the exercises behind and express your vision. You have also developed your roles through the exercises behind. Now work on developing your core values, such as health, top performance in your field, harmony, independence, autonomy, etc. Now enter your core values in the form as shown in Fig. 20.2.

Basic values / Roles	A	B	C	D	E	F
Life-role						
Personal-role						
Work-role						
Societal-role						

Fig. 20.2 Roles and values

In each of the cells, there are two questions to answer

1. What does this mean for me?
2. How do I perform this role?

You answer the questions by grading the answers from 1 to 7, where 7 is the best score and 1 is the worst score.

Development of Top Performance

When we climb in the mountains, we come to a point on the mountainside, usually approximately halfway up, where we evaluate the progress and understand what we have embarked on. This is also the case when we seek to become really good at something. At various times in life, we have made some choices that have become established as the pattern we now operate according to. If we do not make new conscious choices, then as a general rule we will do what we have always done and we will largely achieve the results we have always achieved.

What is it that makes some people achieve mediocre results, while others achieve success or perform at the top level? There seem to be some common features of top performance:

- They are committed to a vision that encompasses more than their own best interests.
- The activities have a purpose.
- The results are measurable.
- You work in teams.
- The course is corrected along the way.
- The leadership style is corrected along the way.
- Momentum and goal focus are maintained.
- One changes in pact with changes in the outside world.
- You have confidence in yourself.

These factors can be represented figuratively as shown in Fig. 20.3

What really makes a difference between those who perform at the top and those who do not is the inner drive. It is the inner motivation that really matters whether one achieves medium results or achieves top performance. It is figuratively our inner mountain peak we must climb to achieve top performance in the outer life.

The feeling of powerlessness seems to inhibit the achievement of top achievements, such as feeling that one has little influence over the development of one's own life. This may, for example, be that you feel that you have little influence on being able to change something that is important for your own career. If you also identify with your own powerlessness, this has a direct negative effect on your level of performance.

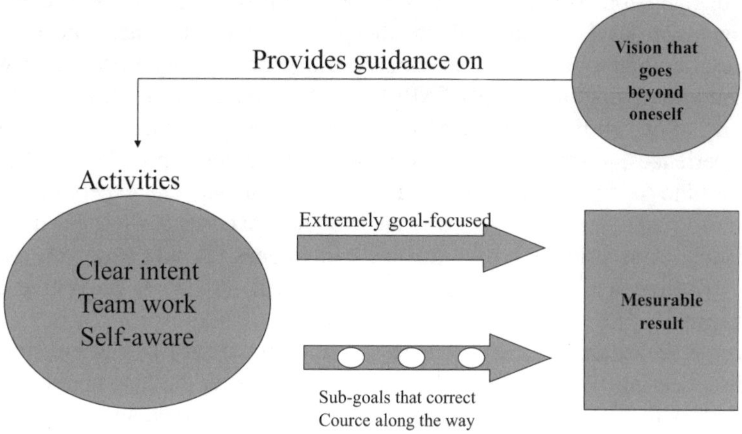

Fig. 20.3 Some common features of people who perform at the top

There are two key variables that are crucial to changing oneself or others from powerlessness and mediocre performance to achieving top performance. First, it's the way you think. Second, something happens when you change the way you think. We experience our experiences and impressions in a new and different way when we change the way we think. This is reviewed in an exercise later in this presentation.

Top performance and a new way of thinking can be linked to a technique called the placebo effect. Placebo is what works, because we think it works. In some experiments in medical science, for example, a sugar pill is used in scientific research instead of a real medicine. Studies have shown that in approximately in 20% of the cases where subjects are given placebo, for example sugar pills, this has positive measurable effects on the subject. In other words, it is the belief that something works that makes it work. The old saying: Faith can move mountains, can have more in it than just a chuckling superiority from a random observer.

The purpose must be to use all conceivable resources to achieve top performance. We must, of course, take moral and ethical considerations into account in this picture. Placebo is a technique that can help many to move from powerlessness, mediocre results to top performance, by starting to think, sense, experience and act differently.

An easy way to get help from placebo—the effect is to adjust to the fact that we are able to solve the problem or challenge we face. The starting point is that if others can solve the problem, so can we. It is to put the thought activity into a mode where we think we are mastering the situation, which in this context is to make use of the placebo effect. We review an exercise later in this presentation where we use the placebo effect.

Once you have reviewed the exercise that is linked to the placebo effect, you have created your own little mental pharmacy. We can call this your personal placebo generator. You can use this to put yourself in a state where you perform at a top level. Remember that the placebo generator that you develop in the exercise should end with a memory word, which is easy to come up with in different situations, for example FARM: satisfied, others' respect, mastery. When you now, after you have completed the exercise, apply the memory rule to everyday experiences, a new level of performance will be developed. This will be your new baseline for future performance. Remember that everyday experiences are not high-performance experiences, but that everyday experiences can be filled with inspiration from your high-performance experiences. In this way, you establish a new baseline for your achievements, which will also apply to your everyday experiences.

Flow is an experiential state where no resistance exists, and where time feels like disappearing. This is achieved as a general rule after the long continuous time you work with a problem or challenge that you are concerned about. Athletes call this condition being in the zone. Jazz musicians call it being 'in the groove'. Flow occurs when we focus all our attention on the present task. Flow is an important prerequisite for achieving top performance; therefore, it is important that you set aside long continuous sessions where you can work with the present problem or challenge.

Exercises

1. Set a personal goal for yourself in your work situation. Examine this goal in the light of the 10 factors to achieve goals.
2. Think of a person you really appreciate and who is a role model for you, such as something you admire for what the person does or has done (historical people, friends, family, from fairy tales, from the world of myths, from religion, etc.).
   a. Choose a goal that your role model achieved by living out his vision. Develop for your inner gaze, your own inner theatre a short film of approximately 30 seconds of this goal. Make the film meaningful and inspiring.
   b. Now step into the role where you are the one who achieves this goal. Make your core values clear to you, your principles and your personal vision.
   c. Now play the film for your inner theatre, where you play the main role and achieve the goal.
   d. When you play this role in the movie, ask yourself the following questions:
      i. What are your motives?
      ii. Why am I doing this?
      iii. How does the goal connect to my vision?
      iv. How does it feel to work towards this goal?
   e. Use the whole of Exercise 2 above when meeting people to reach out for what your role models would have done in a similar situation.

Linking personal achievement to our core values

3. List four goals that are important to you. Then set up the roles that correspond to these goals. How will you shape your personal vision as a result of your goals and roles?
4. Set up at least one work role that is important for you to master. Reflect on how you can use your time more efficiently, not necessarily spend more time, to perform better in this work role.
5. List at least three personal roles that you want to perform better. What can you imagine doing to perform better in these three personal roles. Use tomorrow to improve what you think can be improved. Let it go for a week and make a similar appearance. Now check if you have received feedback that you can use to perform better within these roles.
6. List one and only one societal role that you wish you had performed better in. Spend the next month on a small push to improve your personal performance within this role. At the end of the month, you should evaluate whether you yourself think you have benefited from improving yourself in this role.
7. Fill out the form below. Only the most important roles and your basic values are to be filled.

There are two questions that are asked about the contents of each cell that you have entered. Divide each cell with a diagonal line starting at the top left of each cell and down towards the adjacent diagonal point, as exemplified for life-role and basic value A. Below the line, ask the question: How much does this value mean for me attached to this role? Above the line, ask the question: How well do you perform this value associated with this role? Degrees from 1 to 3 in each of the cells, where 1 is small and 3 is a lot. You have now developed a form for you personally that says something about your roles and your basic values. However, the numbers for these vary and they will probably be different in the different cells. The potential for improvement and for having the buoyancy to reach your goals lies in the cells where the differences are greatest, and where the value means the most to you, for example where you score 3 on what a value means to you in your role, but you score only 1 on how well you perform the value in this role. Now develop a personal strategy to improve the performance of your roles in relation to your core values (Fig. 20.4).

8. Set a goal that you really want to achieve in the near future, let's say 1–2 years. How does this goal fit in relation to the form roles and values above? What role and what value was it that emerged in your goal? Is it this role and this value you identify with?
9. Imagine that you have achieved the goal you set for yourself in task 8.
   a. What do you see in the past?
   b. How do you feel?
   c. What do you hear?
   d. How does this change your roles?
   e. How does this affect your values?

Basic values / Roles	A	B	C	D	E	F
Life-role						
Personal-role						
Work-role						
Societal-role						

Fig. 20.4 Roles and values

10. Imagine that the goal has been reached. Now think about the path you have to take to reach the goal. How did you influence other people to achieve your goal? Imagine walking along the path you had to take to reach your goal. Walk slowly along the road to the goal while imagining how your actions affected you and others along this road. Are the methods you used in accordance with your basic values? Were your roles affected in any way, if so how? Did anyone help you along the way? Have you given these feedback? Was the goal the consequences that met you along the way?
11. Now consider the different goals you have for your life in the future. See these goals in relation to your core values and your roles. How do goals affect your roles and your values?

Development of top performance

12. Think of a situation where you felt particularly powerless. It must be a real event that you remember relatively well. Try to think back. What was it you imagined just before you felt powerless in the current situation? Was it, for example, anger, frustration, despair, aggression, meaninglessness, I do not mind this, this is enough, addiction, etc.?
13. Try to imagine how you would feel if you had tackled the problem, the conflict, the challenge, etc., that made you powerless in task 12, for example upstairs, confident, confident, calm, balanced, satisfied, etc. Keep this picture of you even for approximately one minute. Take all the time you need for this image to develop and attach itself to your retina. Let this picture be real to you.
    a. Now imagine this feeling as a dot in front of you. Let the dot grow and fill the entire room in front of you, and then around you and finally the entire room.
    b. Now move this image of yourself over to the situation you imagined in Exercise 12, where you felt powerless.

c. Let the feeling of powerlessness slowly disappear as the feeling of yourself as one who masters the situation completely erases the feeling of you as powerless.
d. Now imagine several situations of powerlessness and let your feeling of mastering the situation trickle over these feelings of powerlessness.
e. In any situation you encounter in the future, try to deal with these by letting them fill with your feeling where you master situations. This applies to situations that actually occur and situations that you recall from memory or that you imagine in the future.
f. Every time you encounter a situation where you need to perform at the top, put your thinking activity in the position where you felt you mastered the situation. This is like getting into a roundabout with the car and then choosing the right direction out of the roundabout. If there are no signs, it will be difficult to choose the right direction even if you know where you are going. Your sign in any roundabout where you want to master at the top is the feeling where you mastered the situation.

14. Think of a positive experience in your life, once you experienced that you had great creativity, great insight or a very strong concentration around something you focused strongly on achieving. In such a situation, we talk about that one just flows with and that time ceases. This may have happened in sporting activities, on a mountain hike, in love life, at home with the children, at work or the like. What is important to find out is a situation where you were really connected, and where you yourself felt that you made an excellent achievement, an achievement you were really happy with yourself. When you have come to such an experience, step into it mentally and imagine sounds, feel for how you felt, etc. Let this experience persist in your inner theatre for approximately 5 minutes.
    a. Now think of a completely ordinary experience in your everyday life, which did not affect your life in any particular direction, for example reading the morning newspaper, eating breakfast, sleeping dinner rest, drinking morning coffee, etc.
    b. Now compare the two experiences you have evoked in your inner theatre. Find out what the difference is between the two experiences. What is it about one experience that really affected you that you do not find in the other experience? Imagine these main elements in your inner theatre, as if you were making a movie out of these elements. Write down three to five of these main elements, the ones you find in the experience that really influenced you and that have been of great importance to you, such as helping others, achieving something, mastering something fully and getting recognition of others.
    c. Now think of a situation where you felt powerless (e.g. Exercise 12). It must be a real event that you remember relatively well. Now compare the feeling of powerlessness with the feeling of mastery. Play both of these emotions in your inner theatre. Let the feeling of mastery slowly dominate the other feeling. It is this feeling of mastery that you should bring with

you in your future situations, as well as when you remember experiences that you did not master. The point of the latter is not to forget or repress, but to let the experiences come in a different perspective.

d. Now make a simple rule of thumb from the elements that you wrote down in exercise b, such as respect, responsibility and dignity (RAV).
e. The next time you are going to accomplish something, whatever it is, bring out that word and evoke the inner feeling of top performance. Let this feeling irrigate the situation you are in.
f. Now let experiences from your past, which are not particularly pleasant for you to remember, be sprinkled with the feeling of mastery using the simple word you have now developed, by playing this in your inner theatre.
g. Call this word your placebo generator and bring it out as needed. Always keep it easily accessible.

15. Ask yourself the following questions: What do you want to remember from your everyday experiences? These are the experiences that fill most of your life. They may take 90–99% of your time. What do you want to be left with in your memory from this time? Use approximately half an hour on this exercise.

Personal Communication Coaching Tools: Future Images

Explanation of future images
What is a future picture? It is a representation of a future state, which is so realistic and powerful that it affects your performance here and now. Top athletes, for example, have a clear picture of themselves about the achievements of a future sport. When they talk about this, they are detailed and they know how it feels to perform at this level. The image is so effective that it affects their performance here and now.

Development of future images
Future images bring in an expectation mechanism that governs the behaviour here and now. In this way, the future affects the present. Future images give us a taste of the future, the future we want to create for ourselves and others. In this way, future images motivate action. One can imagine such futures quite concretely, hear sounds from the imagined future and feel the feeling of being there.

A concrete example of a future picture is when we pick up next year's travel brochures and imagine next year's holiday. Another example is to imagine what it feels like to master a new skill.

Future images can be used to motivate oneself to achieve results, which one really wants to realize.

Exercise

Imagine something you really want to achieve in a future work context.

- What does this look like?
- How will it feel to have achieved this? Describe this briefly to yourself.
- What comments do you get from the outside world in the imagined future when you have achieved what you wanted?
- What reward will you give yourself when you achieve this?
- Does this future have a sound, an image, a taste or a smell that you can evoke here and now?
- Is it necessary to change something in your everyday life in order for you to achieve the goal?

21 Personal Communication Benchmarking

Aims of this Chapter

1. The purpose of this chapter is to describe the key principles, procedures and strategies of personal communication benchmarking, as understood in this context.
2. In this chapter, the reader should reflect on the following concepts: benchmarking, competence development, thought dispositions, identity and perception.

Diffusion of Competence

The main question in personal communication benchmarking is the following: How does the person who is extremely skilled do it in an area we want to improve in? The point is to excel in this limited area. Personal communication benchmarking can be understood as a way of transferring competence, i.e. knowledge, attitudes and skills. Personal communication benchmarking is based on the idea of continuous competence development.

Personal communication benchmarking can be divided into an inner and an outer focus. It can be further divided into how we orient ourselves in relation to intention and to action. Depending on how we focus and how we orient ourselves in relation to the person we want to model or benchmark ourselves against, it is the other person's linguistic pattern, his or her thought dispositions and his or her behaviour that are modelled.

We have developed a typology for personal communication benchmarking that is intended to make it easier to distinguish between different types of personal communication benchmarking (Fig. 21.1).

K. Ledingham et al., *Rethinking Innovation*,
https://doi.org/10.1007/978-3-031-40848-9_21

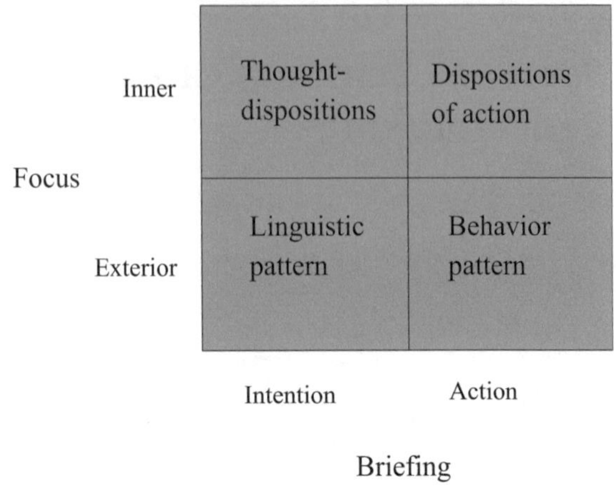

Fig. 21.1 Types of personal communication benchmarking

Depending on the type of personal communication benchmarking you want to do, there is information at several levels, which must be provided. The collection of information can take place in several ways, for example by interview, questionnaire, role play, simulation, interactive engagement, observation, etc.

Levels of Personal Communication Benchmarking

Personal communication benchmarking can be presented in six levels:

- Purpose
- Identity
- Perceptions
- Competence
- Behaviour
- The outside world.

The outside world
The question here is: Where and when is the person you want to model acting? Divide the outside world into two sizes to make it simpler and clearer, the macro-world and the micro-world.

To uncover the macro-world, one asks questions of the type: Are there any general features of the world around which the person you want to model operates? These can be, for example, social structures and processes that can influence the actions of the person you want to model. In order to uncover the micro-world, more specific questions are asked that are intended to reveal the special conditions of the world around which the person you want to model operates.

Behaviour

Here, we are concerned with what the person does, his work pattern and his way of interacting with others, his communication style, etc. There is, for example, a special way in which he handles problems and challenges. Does he have a special work style to achieve the goals he has set? Look first at his macro-behaviour, i.e. his general pattern, and then you concentrate on the micro-journey, which are the very special action patterns he uses, such as specific work routines.

Competence

How does the person use their competence? First look at the macro-competence, i.e. his knowledge, skills and attitudes on a general level. This can be, for example, his learning strategy, his motivational strategy, his creativity and his decision-making strategy. Then concentrate on the micro-competence. This can be his way of visualizing, his internal dialogue and how he uses his senses to filter information.

Perceptions

What perceptions and values does the person make visible? First look at his macro-views. These are the general perceptions and values that are made visible, for example expressed opinions about basic conditions. Then examine the microconceptions. These are perceptions that are more context and situation dependent.

Identity

This is the role that the person holds or the identity he makes visible. Look at the macro-identity first. This deals with the person's identity in relation to the larger system he is part of, for example participation in the political environment. Then examine the role or identity of the person in relation to others in their immediate environment.

Purpose

This says something about what meaning or purpose the person sees with their life. First, examine the macro-purpose, that is, the purpose or meaning he expresses in what he does. Then examine the micro-level, focusing on his personal vision.

In the next section, we look at a method for personal communication benchmarking.

Conscious and unconscious skills

Conscious skills can be described as a function of knowledge in action. The unconscious skills are to be understood so that one can accomplish something with great success without being able to describe or explain to others how to do this. The unconscious skills are part of what is described in the literature as tacit knowledge.

One of the biggest challenges in personal communication benchmarking is that those who are experts often perform their skills on an unconscious level; that is, it is tacit knowledge, which at best is difficult to transfer to others as information. This is often referred to as fingertip feeling, gut feeling, intuition, etc.

Unconscious skills	Conscious skills
Fous on experience Focus on part-whole understanding Focus on contextual understanding Focus on induction Focus on analogy and intuition Approach by role play	Focus on structure focus on analysis focus on objective distance focus on deduction focus on the cognitive focus on digital processes, such as. either-or; logical approach

Fig. 21.2 Benchmarking processes for conscious and unconscious skills

One of the goals of personal benchmarking is precisely to uncover unconscious skills, and make these skills conscious, so that they can be used for personal development. Both the conscious and the unconscious skills can be benchmarked or modelled.

To benchmark the unconscious skills means that one must take the other's position, and see it all from the other's perspective. In this way, the personal intuition develops over time in relation to the other's subjective experiences. This can be done by various forms of master journeyman organization.

Benchmarking the conscious skills means taking a third position, i.e. the perspective of a neutral observer, who in objective terms describes the explicit structure of the personal experiences of the person one wants to model, so that this can be transferred to others.

The two benchmarking processes may, for example, look as shown in Fig. 21.2.

The unconscious skills focus on pattern detection and pattern understanding. The conscious skills focus on systematization and structuring of information. Both of these processes are important to be involved in personal communication benchmarking.

Personal communication benchmarking often requires us to be able to describe the processes and phenomena we want to recreate. To describe different perspectives or positions that a person can take, there are five ways of looking at things that can be applied. The procedure is then to uncover how the person we are going to model or benchmark uses the different perspectives in relation to other people.

First position: This is one's own perspective. One sees situations and events from one's own point of view, and assesses everything from this perspective.

Second position: Here you take the other person's perspective and see the world from his point of view. One tries metaphorically to be in the other's shoes.

Third position: Here one tries to understand how a neutral observer would have assessed the situation.

Fourth position: Here you try to see how the system as a whole is affected by what is happening, as well as how the larger system is affected.
Fifth position: This is the third position, only that now there is a neutral observer who observes how the system as a whole and the larger system are affected.

We now turn to describe the phases of personal communication benchmarking.

The Phases of Personal Communication Benchmarking

When we are going to prepare personal communication benchmarking, we must first select the person we want to model, or benchmark ourselves against. We must also choose the context we want to use for the modelling. You must also clarify when and where you can intervene with the person you want to model. Furthermore, it should be clarified which relationship you want to achieve with the person in question, as well as which condition you prefer to be in when the modelling is to take place.

There are three phases in personal communication benchmarking. The first phase is the information phase. The second phase is model development, and the third phase is the transfer phase.

First phase: Information

One should try to get into a position where the person to be modelled performs the performance you want to model. You immediately take the second position, described above, and try to understand what the person is thinking and feeling while performing the performance. Also try to take in the body language of the other. Concentrate on the macro-level, the small arm movements and the small muscle movements. This enables you to get a little below the surface structures of the other. In this phase, do not try to understand what the person you are modelling is doing. You start from this stage in a state where you do not know what is happening at all. You should try to set aside all previous mental models so that the assumptions and perceptions you may have are not valid in this phase. You start here on bare ground and will build up knowledge from scratch.

When you yourself feel that you have been in this phase long enough, find a context where you can practice doing what the other person did, while trying to think like the other person. Now try to act as if you were the other, while striving for the same result that he achieves. This alternation between being yourself and trying to be like the other will give you a double understanding of the achievement you are trying to benchmark.

You should be observant of the response from the outside world. When the response from the outside world is about the same in the two states, to be oneself and to try to act as if one were the other, then this phase is over.

An auxiliary model for observing the other in this phase is called ROLE (representation system, orientation, links, effects).

Representation system:	This is connected to which of the five senses the person you are to model is dominated by: the visual, the auditory, the tactile, smell or taste. This applies to the person's behaviour, linguistic pattern and his cognitive style.
Orientation:	This is linked to whether the person is internally or externally oriented.
Links:	This is linked to the person's way of thinking and talking. There are two main ways that can be revealed here: a. Linear, i.e. whether the person speaks in a linear cause and effect context. b. Circular, i.e. whether the person thinks and speaks in circular or interactive ways.
Effects:	This is linked to the results the person achieves. Here, we are interested in what it is about the representation system, the orientation and the links that produce these effects.

Phase 2: Simplified model
In this phase, it is important to find out what is essential and what is of less importance for the actual performance you want to model. Your goal in this phase is to clarify the specific cognitive and behavioural characteristics that promote the desired performance. In this phase, you try out different elements to see what works and what does not work. You systematize and structure the elements that have an effect. Anything that has no effect must be removed. This is the simplification process where models become visible and constantly simplified. The purpose here is to bring out the simple model, which has the desired effect. The result of this phase is a mini-model.

A helper model for phase 2 is WOUNDS (symptoms, causes, results, effects, resources).

Symptom:	What are the specific observable or measurable symptoms that should be modelled?
Causes:	What are the causes or causes of these symptoms?
Results:	What short-term results are achieved?
Effects:	What are the more long-term effects achieved?
Resources:	What resources does the person you are modelling have access to?

Phase 3 transfer
The final phase involves designing procedures so that others can learn from what you have modelled. The idea is that by following these procedures, the others should ideally achieve the same performance as the person you modelled did.

Exercises

1. Start with a leader that you want to model.
   a. What is the stated purpose of this person?
   b. What is the vision of this person?
   c. How does he seek to achieve his purpose and vision?
   d. What does he do to correct the course to achieve the purpose and vision?
2. Start with a person you want to model.
   a. Use the five positions to investigate how this person positions himself in relation to others, i.e. how he uses the five positions in his interaction with others.
3. Imagine three people you know relatively well. Consider which of the five positions they often use in the conversations they engage in with other people.
4. Select a person you want to model. Choose what you want to model in this person, such as relationship skills.
   a. Observe what he does and how he does this in relationships with others.
   b. Try to grasp his body language. Then use ROLE (see front) to complete the modelling.
   c. Develop a simple model for what you model in the other. Use WOUNDS (see front).

Personal Communication Coaching Tools: Mirroring

Explanation of mirroring as a personal communication tool
Mirroring is meant to mirror the other person's behaviour. If the other person, for example, speaks fast, walks fast, etc., then the technique is to try to imitate this behaviour. This sounds banal, but imagine walking with a person down a corridor where you are talking. The other person walks fast in the corridor and you walk slowly. Then you take control of the other by forcing him to follow your pace. You take power over the situation by doing this, but you do not mirror the other by doing this. Other examples of concrete mirroring are talking slowly if the other person is talking slowly. In a way, you follow the speed, tempo and tone of the other person in the playing technique.

Mirroring also means that you, for example, notice the other person's arm movements, posture, linguistic expressions such as metaphors, etc. This does not mean that you submit to the other person's behaviour, or behave like a parrot. It is you who takes control of the situation by mirroring the other, not the other way around. Mirroring thus means that through this technique takes control of the situation.

The purpose of the mirror is to create a breeding ground for the good relationships, build consensus on a concrete level and facilitate the communication process between yourself and the person you are mirroring. Mirroring basically means that you show the other person respect and take him seriously. The mirror facilitates the interaction with the other by using concrete techniques. Of course, one must be careful not to imitate the other in a way that seems offensive.

The mirror helps to develop trust and cooperation. If you work together in a team, the mirroring will facilitate the togetherness and the interaction will be easier.

The procedure is to observe the other carefully. Just observing the other creates a situation where the other party feels involved. You should look for posture, facial expressions, facial expressions, arm movements, etc. Listen to how he uses the language, such as tone of voice, metaphors, stories, use of images, etc. By mirroring the other in such a concrete way, without seeming intrusive, you establish a relationship at a specific behavioural level.

Exercise

Try to uncover how others will be able to use the mirroring technique on you. This will provide insight into your own pattern of action, while at the same time you know exactly what to look for in others that you want to mirror. Review the following questions and prepare them for yourself.

a. What arm movements do you use often?
b. How do you stand when talking in a group?
c. Do you have a special tempo or tone of voice when talking to others?
d. Do you interrupt others before they have finished talking?
e. Are there any words you use more often than other words?
f. Do you have any metaphors or models you use often?
g. Do you use the last sentence from your conversation partner as a starting point for the further conversation? This is a classic mirroring technique. One takes as a starting point the last sentence that the other uses, reformulates it so that it is always perceived positively for the other and builds it on further communication based on this. This connects mirroring and harmony in a completely genuine way, and allows you to take control of the situation. In the same way as one talks about the power of definition and model power, one can in such a situation talk about the power of reflection. One literally takes power over the situation by mirror power. It is very effective and is used consciously by people who want to take control of communication processes.
h. Do you hold your hands in any special way when talking to others?
i. Do you sneeze before you start talking?
j. Do you use many words of the type: correct, just to give feedback?

It may be appropriate for two people who know each other relatively well to perform this exercise together.

Personal Motivational Strategy for Communication

22

Aims of this Chapter

1. Too understand personal motivation.
2. In this chapter, the reader should reflect on the following concepts: action strategies, values and criteria.

Motivational Strategy

We divide motivation into inner and outer motifs. Needs, desires and interests are typical examples of inner motive. Reward is an example of an external motive. Personal motivation strategy relates to the steps and operations that people perform to achieve goals and desires. Personal motivation strategy involves performances and visualization. The personal motivation strategy is different ways of encouraging oneself to achieve goals and dreams.

Our values guide the selection of our goals, at the same time as our values influence our action strategies and thus our actions. A model for the personal motivation strategy is shown in Fig. 22.1

Our Values

An essential point of focusing on dreams and goals, and not on the behaviour to get there, is to create an attractor, which draws you towards something. This will stimulate the activity and energy that you need when you envision the goal and dream as realized in an expected future.

Our values can be understood as principles and qualities we strive for, and which have a governing effect on the activities of everyday life. Our values are the

K. Ledingham et al., *Rethinking Innovation*,
https://doi.org/10.1007/978-3-031-40848-9_22

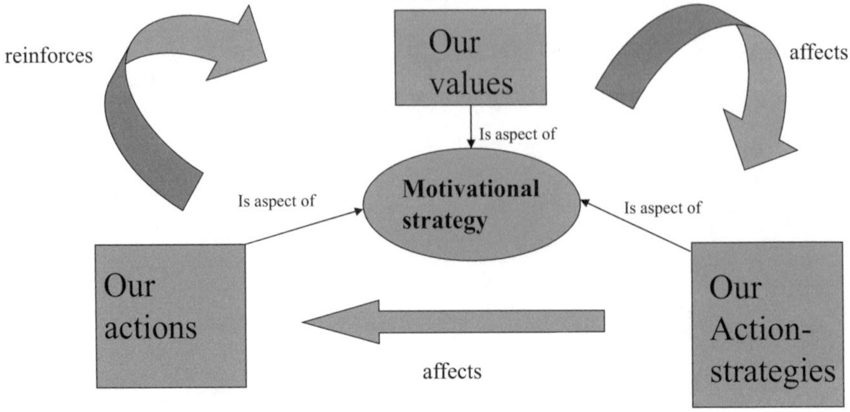

Fig. 22.1 Model for personal motivation strategy

primary source of our motivation. When we live in accordance with our values, we achieve a feeling of well-being, satisfaction, balance and harmony. Then, we know why we do what we do. If, on the other hand, we do not live in accordance with our values, disharmony, imbalance, dissatisfaction and an inner turmoil arise.

To examine your own values, take the time to answer the following questions:

- What is it that basically motivates you?
- What is especially important to you in your life?

Some of your possible answers may be linked to success, to gaining the attention of others, to learn something new, to be allowed to take responsibility, to be accepted, to be allowed to please others, to achieve something you appreciate, to be allowed to create something, etc.

The goals we set for ourselves are an expression of our values. A person who has stability as one of his fundamental values will set goals that are related to this value. Such a person will seek other goals than a person who values, e.g. autonomy.

A person seeking stability is likely to be happy with a 9–4 job, steady income and predictable tasks. A person seeking autonomy will probably try to find a job that is not so predictable and secure, such as starting their own business.

Our goals can metaphorically be seen as values we have placed in a future that we want to realize. A person's values will also affect how that person assesses a particular situation. A person who values safety will tend to consider situations in relation to possible dangers associated with the situation. A person who values challenges may in the same situation look for opportunities to create something.

Values are often associated with criteria, but they are not synonymous concepts. Value relates to what we strive for and want to achieve. Criteria refer to the standards we use when we make decisions to achieve our values (Fig. 22.2).

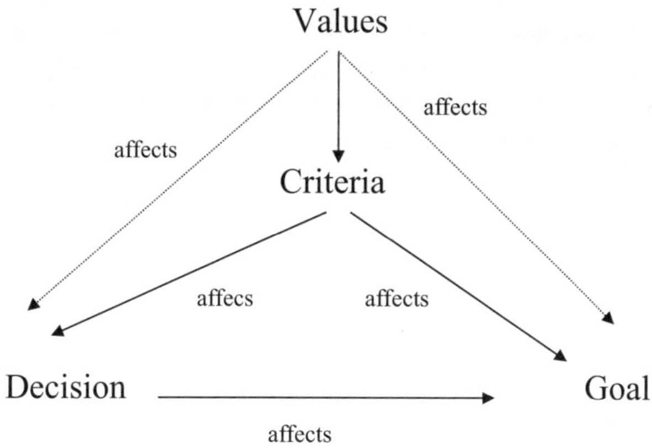

Fig. 22.2 Values, criteria, decision and goals

The criteria and values must match; otherwise, internal tension can easily arise, which will inhibit motivation. Our values are a classic example of our subjective experiences, contrasted with facts, which can be understood as objective, in the sense that they are possible to test.

Two people who say they have the same values or system of values can act completely differently in the same situation. This may be because their criteria are different even though they have the same value base. The difference between someone's values and their criteria is therefore a very important distinction, to be able to say something about how they can be thought to act in a particular situation. Therefore, their action strategy for achieving the goals may be different; that is, they use different means to achieve the same goal. The story is full of examples of this. How often do we not hear: We have the same goal, but we use different means to get there. Then, it is the criteria, the standards used, that are most likely different. For example, two people may have the value of respect in common. On the other hand, they can act completely differently in the same situation, where respect as value is made visible. This is because they have different criteria or standards in relation to what leads to or what they believe is respect. Respect as a value can motivate action, but actions can be completely different.

The relationship between value and criterion often arises when different cultures meet. This applies at the individual level, at the group level, at the organizational level and at the societal level.

At the organizational level, this is expressed, for example, when two organizations are merged through acquisitions or the like. This is becoming increasingly relevant in the global economy. At the individual level, the relationship between value and criterion is expressed in geographical movements and encounters with new customs and norms.

The hierarchy we organize our values and our criteria according to relates to the degree of importance or meaning that we attach to different actions and experiences. An example of a hierarchy of criteria is a person who puts health above financial success. Such a person will be motivated more by promoting their own health rather than achieving financial success. He will probably structure his life more around physical activities than professional challenges. A person with opposite criteria would have a different lifestyle. Clarifying people's value hierarchy is therefore crucial to knowing what motivates them.

Value hierarchy and hierarchy of criteria arise because there are different types of values that have different functions. There are four types of values that we describe in the following:

- The values that are a means to achieve other goals, such as money.
- The values that are goals in themselves, such as harmony.
- The values that are both means and goals, such as health.
- Core values, such as well-being.

The different types of values will motivate us in different ways in relation to strength and intensity.

Core values are the values that come closest to a person's or organization's purpose or meaning. The answer to the following questions is the core value that governs your life, or for an organization: What is the purpose of what you are doing? The core value is expressed at a strategic level as something we want to achieve. We must always ensure that over time there is a balance between our process values and the result values. If such a balance does not exist, statements of the type: The goal sanctifies the means, distort our entire value base and our criteria, i.e. the standards we use in our lives. The goals can easily be changed to match the means we use, to create a psychological balance. The same balance must also exist between the level of action and the level of strategy. If such a balance does not exist, it could be expressed in inconsistency, i.e. we do not do what we say we will do.

Most systems are organized around a few core values. The hierarchy of these core values, i.e. purpose, identity, attitudes, competence and behaviour, provides an important insight into the motivation structure of both individuals and systems.

Values and criteria reveal a good deal of how the individual thinks, as well as how he responds to the expressed values of others. One way to examine and uncover motivational structures for people is to find the system of values they relate to. A system of values is the framework in which all people are part of, and which influences their motive for acting the way they do. We have developed a simple value matrix based on the most important relationships we enter into (Fig. 22.3).

The value matrix is assumed here to be the key to the individual's motivation. Common values are also assumed to be the glue that holds different social systems together. Value conflicts are believed to be the source of disharmony and tensions within and between social systems. This can easily paralyse the motivation of

Relationships / Value- hierarchy	Work		At home		Society	
	Means	core value	Means	core value	Means	core value
Purpose						
Identity						
Attitudes						
Competence						
Behavior						

Fig. 22.3 Value matrix

the individual and the system as a whole. Such value conflicts can metaphorically function as a mental virus, just as computer viruses or biological viruses can destroy physical and organic systems.

From a management perspective, it is crucial that we clarify the value system of the individual, because these are the areas the person is motivated in relation to. A person's value matrix will have a governing effect on his motivational structure and be fundamental for the development and change of his mental models or his mental map.

Our Action Strategies

Our overall action strategies say something about how we approach a problem, a challenge, an opportunity, etc. The following action strategies are not mutually exclusive. They are general and say something about how we are motivated in given situations. The most well-known action strategies are as follows.

Approach to a problem

- against what is positive
- away from the negative

Source of inspiration

– inner
– outer

- Initiative
  - proactive (future oriented)
  - reactive (historically oriented)
- Reflection style
  - vision oriented
  - action oriented
  - logically oriented
  - emotionally oriented

The following form can be used to uncover your own and others' action strategies. The purpose in this context is to gain insight into how to motivate in creative situations. That's why we've included Walt Disney's method for developing creativity. In short, it involves taking on different roles, the role of the dreamer, the role of the realist and the role of the critic (Fig. 22.4).

The different action strategies will always be linked to different values for different types of tasks. Linked to creative thinking, it may make sense in the brainstorming phase to let the dreamer's strategies be dominant. When you move from brainstorming to the next phase where you have to evaluate the different ideas, you can let the action strategies of the realist and then the critic be dominant. This approach can be used by the individual and by a team to promote motivation and creative thinking.

Creative strategy / Action-strategy	The Dreamer	The Realist	The Critic
Approach to a problem	Against the positive	Against the positive	Away from the negative
Source of inspiration	Inner.	Exterior	Exterior
Initiative	Proactive	Reactive	Reactive
Reflection style	Vision and emotion	action.	Logical

Fig. 22.4 Form for action strategies in creative situations

Exercises

1. Imagine that you have already achieved a dream or a goal you have set for yourself. Both the goal and the dream correspond to your basic values. Try to visualize this dream or goal. What do you see? What do you hear? What do you feel?
2. Now change the performance so that you play out the dream in your inner theatre. Apply colours to the images you envision. Give some pictures a stronger colour than others and vice versa. Also add sound to your inner theatre so you can hear what's going on there. Now express in words what you see and hear, so that an outsider can imagine this as vividly as possible.
3. What values would you say are your core values?
4. What means will you use to achieve these values?
5. List three of what you would call your core values. For each of these core values, answer the following questions.
   a. What is the purpose of this value in your life?
   b. How does this value affect your identity and your role in relation to other people?
   c. How does this value affect your attitude or perception of others?
   d. How does this value affect your own competence development?
   e. How does this value affect your behaviour?
   f. Are there any contexts this value is more or less appropriate than in other contexts?
6. Identify a core value that is important to you and that you would like to strengthen in yourself. Write down this core value. Then complete the following sentence: This core value is important to me, because ______________ ___________.
7. Also complete the following sentence: This core value is important to me when I ______________________. This is the situation this core value is important to you we are looking for here.
8. What values do you want others to associate you with?
9. What type of competence is important to have and develop in order to strengthen the core value you want others to associate with you?
10. What activities in your life best express the value you want others to associate with you?
11. In what environment or contexts is it the value you want others to associate you with that the value can best be expressed in? Do you seek out these contexts to learn?
12. The form of creative action strategy, where would you say you have a strength, as a dreamer, as a realist or as a critic?
13. In the statements below, put a cross for the statement you feel characterizes yourself best when you communicate with others. It's not necessarily the way you know you should communicate, but the way you mostly communicate, you should tick. If more than one statement in each group is right for you,

tick both statements. The purpose of this exercise is to try to find out where you have a dominance in relation to the action strategies.

Problem approach: The purpose of effective communication is mainly to:

a. avoid conflicts in the relationship
b. develop a good and lasting relationship
c. avoid that we make mistakes when we reach our goals
d. achieve our positive goals
(a and c are motivated by avoiding the negative, while b and d are motivated by the positive).

14. Now reconcile what you answered to problem 15 with problem 13.
15. Now rank from 1 to 5 the areas that you think are most important to emphasize when communicating with others (1 is least important and 5 is most important to you). If you think it all depends on the context in question, then decide on a specific context before you rank the different part statements.
    a. achievement of goals
    b. effective communication
    c. to agree
    d. to learn
    e. to share knowledge
    f. to develop new knowledge
    g. to convince others
    h. to present one's own views
    i. to help the other to express his views
    j. to promote the quality of communication
    k. other.
16. Now put the areas you have ranked in order of priority and reflect on which values they correspond to in your value hierarchy.
17. In a communication context (choose which one), put plus (+) for the areas you find easy to perform and minus (-) for the areas you find difficult to perform.
    a. to present something to a larger group
    b. to interview persons
    c. to negotiate
    d. to persuade
    e. to discuss
    f. to lead a light conversation (small talk).

Your orientation says something about what motivates you and what does not motivate you in relation to a communication context.

18. In the statements below, put a cross for the statement you feel characterizes yourself best when you communicate with others. It's not necessarily the way you know you should communicate, but the way you mostly communicate, you should tick. If more than one statement in each group is right for you,

tick both statements. The purpose of this exercise is to try to find out where you have a dominance in relation to the action strategies.

a. Problem approach: The purpose of effective communication is mainly to:
   1. Avoid conflicts in the relationship
   2. Develop a good and lasting relationship
   3. Avoid making mistakes when reaching our goals
   4. Achieve our positive goals

      (1 and 3 are motivated by avoiding the negative, while 2 and 4 are motivated by the positive).
b. Initiative: When I communicate with others, I think it is very important to focus on:
   1. What will happen in the future
   2. What we can learn from the past
   3. What is happening here and now

      (1 is oriented towards the proactive, 2 towards the reactive and 3 is a balance between the two).
c. Source of inspiration: When I communicate it is important for me to
   1. Maintain my own perspective and my opinions
   2. See things from the other person's perspective

      (1 is oriented towards an inner source of inspiration, while 2 is oriented towards an outer source of motivation).
d. Reflection style: When I really want to convey something to someone, then
   1. I try to create an image of the message
   2. I try to be as logical as possible
   3. I'm trying to point out what we need to do to make this happen
   4. I try to make them feel what I really mean

      (1 is related to the visionary, 2 to the logical, 3 to action and 4 to the emotional).

Personal Communication Coaching Tools: Consensus

Explanation of consensus

By consensus here we mean results of you with your behaviour and your words show that you understand and accept the value that other people's experiences have for them. You meet the other literally in their interpretation of situations and events in everyday life. By doing this, you create the basis for good interaction and good communication.

Understanding and accepting do not necessarily mean that you agree with them, but you show that you respect their interpretation of the world. Consensus promotes the foundation of good communication. Once this basis has been developed, many of the possible conflicts that may arise later in the communication process will be easier to deal with.

Showing that you care about the other person in situations where this person needs your help is a simple but very effective way to form the basis for unity. Asking others in different situations what can be done to help them is also an easy way to lay the groundwork for consensus.

Being consistent, letting the other person know where you are in different situations is also an easy way to develop harmony. Remembering what is important to the other and acting accordingly creates the basis for unity. There may be very simple things that the other person perceives as important, but these simple things can have major consequences for the interaction, if you are able to remember and act in accordance with them. Be aware that what seems like a trifle to you may be what triggers the other person's biggest obligation, if you emphasize this with some attention. The little attention can be what triggers the big consequences in a later situation where the interaction is absolutely crucial for you.

Consensus can affect your influence in many situations. It is crucial to be conscious of consensus when disagreeing with someone. Maintaining a good relationship is often more important than presenting your disagreement in a way that may offend the other.

For example, if you are in a situation where you want someone to open up to show more of themselves, but you understand that the person has a bad self-image, then consensus is an important intervention to build the foundation for the good interaction and the good communication at a later time. Showing that you understand and accept the value of the other's experiences creates a situation where the other feels more comfortable in your presence, which is the basis for relationship building, interaction and good communication.

Exercise

A simple exercise for practising consensus is to ask a work colleague what you can do to make his work day nice. Only the question itself helps to develop consensus between you. You do not necessarily have to do anything at all. In most cases, it turns out that the question in itself triggers unanimity between you.

Personal Communication Mastery 23

Aims of this Chapter

1. To understand the prerequisites for personal communication mastery.
2. To understand different focus areas for personal communication mastery.
3. To understand a method for achieving personal communication mastery.

Prerequisites for Personal Communication Mastery

There are four prerequisites for personal communication mastery. These can be referred to as:

- Relationships based on responsibility and trust
- Knowing what you want
- Attention to the outside world
- Flexible behaviour

There is much empirical evidence to support the assumption that relationships based on trust and responsibility are a necessary prerequisite for personal productivity. Personal success always seems to be linked to such relationships. The explanation can be so simple that in such a network, the entire system operates as an organic unit for the benefit of the community. Being associated with such an organic unit will always give greater performance for the individual, than if you had to perform all the activities yourself. It is a classic win–win situation that such an organic entity develops. In our individualistic age, however, there are few such organic networks, because most people will think about what benefits their own success, and not understand or understand that their own success is precisely due to the success of the network they are part of.

K. Ledingham et al., *Rethinking Innovation*,
https://doi.org/10.1007/978-3-031-40848-9_23

Both at the individual level, and in close small social networks based on trust and mutual responsibility, success will presuppose that you have clearly defined what you want to achieve. There are five help questions you should answer to clarify the goal.

1. What do I want to achieve?
2. What do the others in the network want to achieve?
3. What is my goal?
4. What is the goal of the others in the network?
5. How can I help others in the network achieve their goals?

Both relationships based on trust and responsibility for others, as well as knowing what you want, presuppose that you are able to develop attention towards others. In practice, this means something as concrete as listening to what the other person is saying without interrupting, learning to see and sense the other's needs, feeling a change in mood, etc.

Being extremely alert means using all your senses to examine what is happening in a particular situation, both with yourself and with others. Try to be aware of the situations you often slip into when very specific situations arise. This can be irritability, anger, frustration, feeling neglected, etc. Is the condition you often slip into comfortable for you? If the answer is yes, then this is not a problem for you. If the answer is no, then you should do something about it.

The three prerequisites described above are based on being able to exercise flexible behaviour. The thinking is that the more choices one has available for one's behaviour, the greater the room for manoeuvre, and the greater the probability of success. A basic rule here is therefore to change the action alternatives until you find the combination or combinations that lead to the goal. We have shown these four prerequisites for personal success in Fig. 23.1.

Focus Areas for Personal Communication Mastery

There are five focus areas for personal communication mastery we will describe in the following. These focus areas are: the relationship to the outside world, behaviour, skill, perceptions and values as well as identity.

The outside world is here understood as the local environment we relate to, and the people we relate to in this local environment. It is the community we develop in this world that creates circumstances for personal communication mastery far beyond this world.

The behaviours practised in this world are designed to achieve certain purposes. The skills we have developed have often become automatic and part of our unconscious way of being. We largely use these skills without reflecting on the consequences of them. Our skills and behaviour are closely related to our perceptions and values. Our perceptions and values emerge if we ask the questions: What is important to me? What is important for the community I am part of? Our

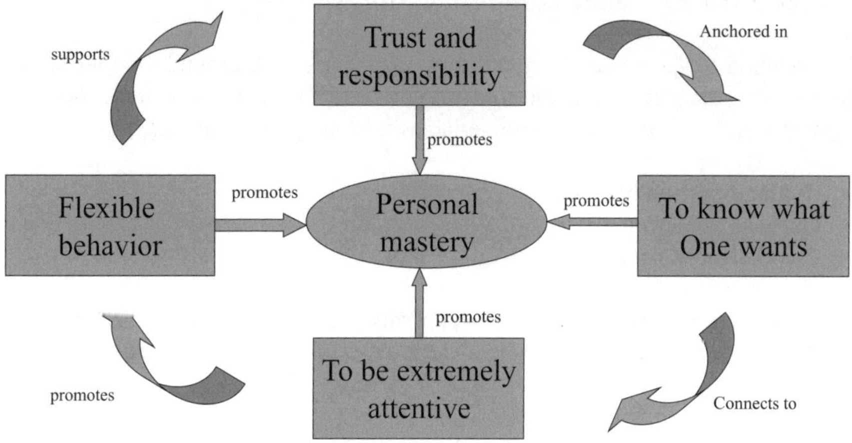

Fig. 23.1 The four prerequisites for personal mastery success

perceptions and values largely control our lives. The question we often ask ourselves is: Why do I do what I do? The answer to this question is almost without exception linked to our values. Our values are directly related to our identity, what sets us apart from others. Identity is our understanding of ourselves in relation to the outside world. The five focus areas for personal communication mastery are shown in Fig. 23.2.

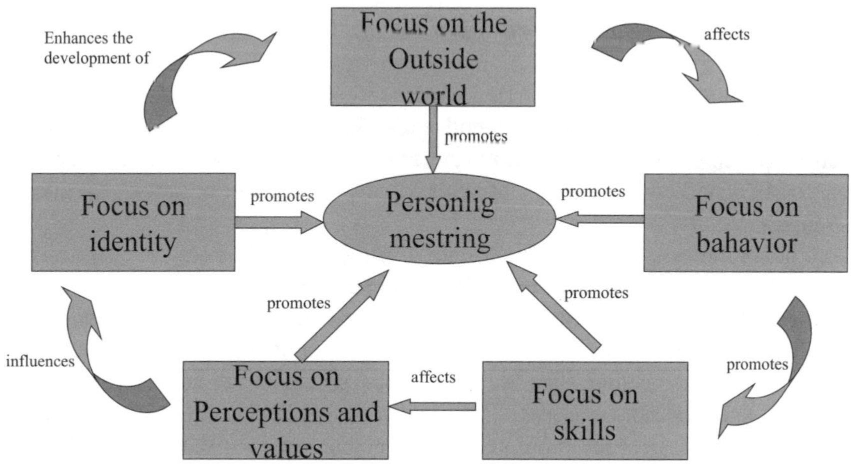

Fig. 23.2 The five focus areas for personal communication mastery

Method for Personal Communication Mastery

The method for personal communication mastery is built around the four prerequisites for personal communication mastery and the five focus areas. We have systematized and structured these variables into three main factors. These are:

- Our way of thinking
- Our goal achievement
- Our pursuit of success

How we think makes the difference that really matters to how we experience what we think. We assume here that there are three main ways of thinking.

- Visually, i.e. thinking in pictures.
- Linguistic, i.e. thinking in text and sounds.
- Emotional, i.e. thinking with the emotions.

The way we think is expressed in the way we communicate. Some communicate mostly in images and metaphors. Others communicate in text, while others communicate with emotions.

In addition to the way we think and communicate, it is important that we renew the mental map we have of reality as our experiences come to. If we do not renew our mental maps when new experiences come, we will spend too many resources on achieving the goals we want to achieve.

When we know how we think and communicate, it will be easier to understand how others think and communicate. In this way, one can approach the others, by communicating more as they do, thus creating greater unity. This will promote self-mastery, because one will be more easily understood by the other. With this procedure, both parties will experience satisfaction in the communication situation. However, only you can take the initiative and decide how you want to react to the actions of others. The best way is always to react in accordance with how the other party thinks and communicates, because it brings a moment of agreement into the situation.

It is not the case that our mental state is stable. It changes continuously according to the situations we come up in. What changes our state we can call an anchor. These anchors can be internal or external. Internal anchors can be experiences you recall from memory when you encounter a new situation. Our state then tends to appear as the mental state we had in the situation the anchor connects to. External anchors can be music. These anchors function in the same way as the internal anchors, i.e. they promote conditions that are not necessarily compatible with personal communication mastery.

The first practical step is to become aware of which anchors change one's mental state. The second practical step is to design your anchor yourself, so that you can consciously change your mental state in the desired direction. Failure to do so drives one into states that can easily impede personal communication mastery. Using anchor to change one's mental state is the key to personal communication mastery.

Exercises

1. Given your basic mental state, i.e. the state you often return to. Give this state a name that you recognize and that is easy to remember, such as irritability, frustration, joy, etc. Also give the desired mental state a name. If there is a coincidence between the desired condition and your basic condition, you do not need to perform this exercise.
    i. What is the difference between the desired mental state and the basic state?
    ii. How can you imagine that this gap can be filled?
    iii. Start with an anchor that you can use to reach the desired state in different situations.
2. Imagine a real event that was problematic in your past. What images, sounds, emotions, smells and tastes appear? Try to imagine a 'movie clip' of this incident, as it could unfold if the circumstances were really bad. Once you have done this, give yourself time to feel how you feel.
3. Imagine a real event that brought joy to your past. What images, sounds, emotions, smells and tastes appear? Try to imagine a 'movie clip' of this incident, as it could unfold if the circumstances were really good. Once you have done this, give yourself time to feel how you feel.
4. Imagine an everyday task that you find difficult or troublesome to perform. Think through the entire sequence of activities with this everyday task. How do you go about making this a success? How do you envision a situation where you perform this task successfully? Hold this image for approximately 5 minutes.
5. The next time a negative event occurs, or a negative memory occurs, think about how you need to perform to make this a success story.
6. Bring to mind a situation where you had a strong sense of satisfaction with what you did. Immerse yourself in the situation.
    i. How do you feel?
    ii. What do you hear?
    iii. What do you see?
7. Imagine yourself in a future situation that you know you do not thrive in. Try to bring with you that feeling of satisfaction from task 6 in the future uncomfortable situation.
    a. Highlight three to four characteristics of the feeling of satisfaction, such as laughter, smiles, positive feedback, etc. Bring these characteristics with you into new situations that arise, and which are not so pleasant.

Personal Coaching Tools in Communication: Involvement-Distancing

Explanation of Involvement-distancing
What is involvement and distancing? There are two main ways to structure our experiences. Involvement happens when we are connected to what happens to all our senses. Distancing occurs when we consider what is happening as if it were far from ourselves, despite the fact that we are a part of it.

Involvement and distancing
When we are involved, we are emotionally engaged. When we are distanced, the emotions are not activated in the same way. In a way, we become observers of what is happening.

If the involvement evokes positive emotions, it does us good. If the involvement is linked to negative emotions, it can hinder our development.

Distancing can be useful if we want to use it to disconnect from a situation for a shorter period of time.

An example of involvement is when you tell someone about an experience you have had, and you notice that you are emotionally upset and engaged while telling.

An example of distancing is when you only describe an experience without engaging in the story itself.

If you want to get involved in something, or want to help others get involved, then involvement can be used as a method. If you want to get mental distance to something, for example when it is required that you think calmly and strategically, then the distance technique can be used.

There are four basic ways to get involved and distanced:

- You get involved in both positive and negative experiences.
- You distance yourself from both positive and negative experiences.
- You are involved in negative experiences and distanced from positive experiences.
- You are involved in positive experiences and distanced from negative experiences.

It can be useful to know if you or others tend to be most involved or most distant from the outside world.

Exercise

Imagine a future situation where your career is at stake. Imagine that in this situation you are engaged and involved with all your senses. Find out how you want to set up the strategy to reach your goal in such a situation. Then try to distance yourself from the same situation by looking at it cold and calm with a basis in facts, key figures, etc. Find out how you want to set up the strategy to achieve your goals.

Personal Communication Identity

24

Aims of this Chapter

1. To understand the impression you want the other or the others to have of yourself.
2. To understand that as a general rule it takes about 3 minutes before the other part(s) have made up a 90% impression of you.
3. To understand that the first impression means a lot, and it takes a lot of energy to change this first impression.

How We Present Ourselves to Others

Be aware that it takes approx. 3 seconds before he or she has formed an 80% perception of you. Also be aware that approx. 93% of the information they or others receive comes from what you do not say.

Johari's window, which was developed by two psychologists, can be an important tool to reflect on when we present ourselves to others. When we are going to create our personal reputation, it is important to be aware of all the panes in Johari's window. These routes are:

- What everyone sees
- Only you can see for yourself
- Only what others see
- What no one sees

As an analogy to Johari's window, we have developed the PCI (personal communication identity) window, which we discuss in the following (Fig. 24.1).

K. Ledingham et al., *Rethinking Innovation*,
https://doi.org/10.1007/978-3-031-40848-9_24

Fig. 24.1 The PCI window

What You are Trying to Show to others	What others Thing of You
What You do not Want to show To others	Personal Communication identity

What You Are Trying to Show to Others

Here, it is important that you try to reflect on what you think you are trying to present by yourself to new people the first three seconds and in the first three minutes you meet. Think carefully about three things that you always try to show to new people you meet.

1. —
2. —
3. —

A good way to find out how to immediately profile yourself is to examine how you yourself react as a customer. The next time you buy something, try to pay attention to the sales process. How do you sell yourself as a customer? Do you have an automatic demeanour, or do you change your demeanour depending on how the others meet you? What makes you happy as a customer?

Bid number 1 when you want to profile yourself is to ask yourself the following questions: What is it that you want to profile yourself when you sell an idea or an argument to others? When you sell an argument or an idea, you usually sell emotions. You connect to other people's feelings and you show your own feelings. You must therefore know what emotions you want to attach to, and you must fully believe in the idea or argument you are going to sell. If this does not happen, it will be seen through, if nothing else, on an unconscious level through the body language you convey. It is your feelings and your commitment that sell in, not necessarily the idea or the argument.

Bid number 2 when profiling yourself is to pay attention to the individual, not to the congregation as a collective group. The question here is: What feelings do you want the other person or others to be left with when you are done? Here you start with the feeling you want to be left with when, for example, the meeting is over, and then you work your way forward in time from this feeling. You therefore decide what feeling the other person will be left with when, for example, the meeting is over, and then take this feeling as a starting point at the beginning of the meeting.

What You Do Not Want to Show to Others

Here, you should do consciously for yourself what you do not want to show to others in your first encounter with them. Think carefully about three things that you do not want to show to new people that you meet.

1. ——
2. ——
3. ——

Be aware that we tend to learn from differences, while we are attracted to similarities, as it is stated in the statement: Equal children play best.

We represent the world through our senses, visually, verbally, emotionally, smell and taste. However, we do not know at the first meeting how the other represents the world, i.e. what emphasis he or she places on the different ways of representing the world. We should therefore present ourselves through as many of our senses as possible in the first meeting. At a later time, you make visible how you yourself represent the world around you, for example visually through the use of images, metaphors, etc.

If we ourselves think in pictures and the other thinks verbally, then conflict can easily arise if we do not take this into account in the first meeting. The first thing you need to do is make yourself aware of how you represent the world around you. As the meeting progresses, pay attention to how one or the other represents the outside world, and then connect to this. Take your starting point in the other person's or other's way of representing the world around you and the desired feeling you want the other person to be left with at the end of the meeting. These are the two rules of action in the part of the PCI window that is called what you do not want to show others, because you then manage to hide what you do not want to show and you connect to positive strings in the other party.

What the Other Thinks About You

Ask for feedback from someone you know well, and whom you trust, if the other person thinks about you. Does what you are trying to show agree with what others perceive? What matches and what does not match? Conversation with the person you are asking for feedback on how you can best match what others think of you and what you want to show of yourself.

We note that the balance between attention to others and openness about yourself can easily lead to one being perceived as friendly, listening, positive, easy to get along with, etc. Attention to others can be achieved by simple banal techniques, such as using the other person's name, to ask questions about the other's life, to show interest in the other's opinions, to make room for the other, etc.

Study the following sentences and look at what nuances you experience:

- I want to start on Monday.
- I would like to start on Monday.
- I need to start on Monday
- I have to start on Monday.
- I should start on Monday.
- I can start on Monday.
- I will start on Monday.

Reflect on the differences in precision and meaning content in the different sentences, which occur only by changing one word. How do you imagine a recipient will perceive the different sentences? Then prioritize the different sentences in the degree of importance that an intended recipient evaluates the different sentences for if, for example, you have been given a job. Do the intentions in the sentences change when we change the words in the sentences? Are there any of the sentences that seem more motivating and positive than the others? Bring out the sentence that you think will have the greatest positive impact on a recipient, and discuss this in a group of three to five people. Take all the necessary prerequisites that you think are necessary to solve such a task.

If someone uses one of the eight sentences or similar statements, and you have to answer them, then an effective way would be to use mirroring technique, i.e. to take as a starting point what they say and then rewrite the sentence in their own words. For example: I want to start on Monday. Why do you want to start on Monday? How do you want us to —? What do you want us to —? This technique has proven to have a great effect in practical situations, because one achieves coherence in communication. The prerequisite for using this technique is that you listen to what the other person is saying, and then intervene with the words they emphasize, because it is probably the words that have the greatest significance for the other person in the current situation.

In order to have an influence on what the other person should think of you after the end of the meeting, it is a crucial quality to learn to listen. Listening also means looking at what the other person is doing when he is talking. The meaning comes out as much in what the other person does when he speaks, as in the words he uses. Therefore, it is paradoxical to use the eyes when listening, just as important as to sharpen only the ears.

In your next meeting with another person, try to find out what key words he uses in his message. At the same time, try to see if he emphasizes the key word with any facts. Then use these facts or movements at the same time as you are based on the key words that the other person uses, without in any way acquiring a parrot behaviour. If you develop this technique, you will build a new way of listening into any communication, where the eyes are just as important as the ears.

Personal Communication Identity (PCI)

So listening means a lot more than using your ears. You should use your eyes as much as you listen. You should listen for the key words that the other person is emphasizing. The images and metaphors that the other uses you should mirror, i.e. take as a starting point when you respond to his statements. At the same time, you should be aware of how he uses arms and facts to reflect this. The point is to achieve unanimity not to imitate the other person's behaviour.

In your listening position, you should pay special attention to words and expressions that may have different meanings, because these can be interpreted in different ways. A lot of skin disagreement arises precisely when one interprets words and expressions in a different way than what the other person meant by these words and expressions. Other words are ambiguous and only make sense if you know or understand the context or know the story behind it.

Ambiguity can arise at different levels:

- the words
- the sentences
- where to put characters in the sentence
- the tone
- body language, etc.

A classic example of a sentence that changes meaning is the following: Do not shoot, wait until I come. Shoot him, do not wait until I come. This sentence is classic, because it can form the basis for a whole series of sentences of the same type.

- Pay him, do not wait until I sign
- Do not pay him, wait until I come
- Do not go, wait until I come
- Go, do not wait until I come
- Get married, do not wait for me
- Do not get married, wait until I come, etc.

Now try to develop three types of sentences within your context, which would have decisive consequences, if you move the comma in the way done above.

Your voice and your body language mean a lot to how you affect others. As a rule of thumb, voice and body language make up over 90% of how you influence others.

Pay special attention to the fact that you seem interested and engaged if you:

- Make eye contact
- Smile
- Listen actively

This shows that you take time for the other, which is a scarce commodity in our time. In the same way as all in-demand shortage goods, participation is greatly appreciated. Also be observant that you seem open and participative if you smile and introduce yourself relatively quickly and in a personal way. If you listen with the same enthusiasm as you talk about yourself and at the same time show empathy with facial expressions and gestures, then the impression increases that you are open and participatory towards others.

If you want to show that you are comfortable with the situation you are in, then the following techniques have proven effective in practice.

- Be energetic
- Speak clearly and distinctly with moderate energy
- Do not come to the conclusion too quickly
- Make eye contact when talking and listening
- Engage everyone in the dialogue
- Tell what you mean without sounding too dominant, i.e. show authority without sounding instructive
- Do not take criticism personally, even if it is meant to be personal.

Be aware that the eyes always reveal you. When someone is angry or aggressive, the eyes 'lock'. If you want to use your eyes to reach the other, keep in mind that you really want to help the other, while trying to understand the other. Keep this thought very clear to you when you speak and listen, because this will be reflected in your eyes and your body language.

When speaking in slightly larger gatherings, try to make eye contact with as many people as possible. A simple technique is to leave a sentence, an idea, etc. connect to each person you make eye contact with. When you do this, you seem more dynamic, engaged and perceived as a person who participates with all of you. Be aware that direct eye contact can be threatening to anyone. One technique here is to fix the gaze on the whole face, not directly on the eyes of the other. This will make it easier for you to make eye contact, and for the other not to get into a position where he feels dominated or threatened.

If someone attacks you with arguments, then do not look down, because it seems like resignation. The judo technique is an effective technique to use here. The judo technique means using the other person's energy and then turning it towards him. For example, you could say the following: 'How would you have done it?', or 'Let's take a closer look at the question or statement', or 'This is a very interesting observation, let's go deeper into it'. Of course, the observation does not have to be interesting or deep, but it always is when you say it is interesting, and goes in depth in the further investigation. This will ease the pressure on the other, and you will take control of the situation.

When someone talks to you, you should not look to the side, because it seems as if you are completely uninterested in what is being said. One can understand the other without having to fall into the trap of accepting what is said or done. Giving unequivocal feedback on understanding what the other person is saying or thinking is, as a general rule, good enough in most situations. Few people demand acceptance for what they do or say, but most desperately want to be understood, because this is something fundamentally human in any communication.

Lean forward towards the other when he speaks, because this shows that you are engaged and shows interest in what he says. If you sit and at the same time support your chin with your hand, you also show great interest. This is an expression of active listening, which affects how the other person perceives you. Do not overdo it, it only leads to ridiculousness or kink in the neck.

As a rule of thumb, if you want to keep people at an arm's length distance, then cross everything without your eyes, such as crossing your hands in front of your chest. You signal either arrogance or insecurity at such an arm movement. At first glance, arrogance and insecurity may seem like two opposites, but are psychologically close.

If you want to appear relaxed and free in a situation, then the following can be some simple steps you can take:

- Wear as little as possible
- Relax your shoulders
- Be straight in the back without blowing out the chest
- Be relaxed at the hips
- Keep your head straight on your shoulders
- Do not move closer than an arm's distance. (This distance literally applies to Northern Europe. In Southern Europe this distance is slightly smaller.) If you get closer than this distance, you seem aggressive.

Imagine a thread from the top of your head and vertically up on the North Star, which pulls your head up from your shoulders. Our posture is controlled from the position of the head. If it seems light and free on the shoulders, the rest of the posture will follow.

The significance of space is important to understand. The intimate zone (approx. 0–0.5 m) is the zone for those closest to us. The private zone (0.5–1.2 m) is the zone for an arm's length distance. The social zone (1.2–3 m) is the zone where the regular meetings take place. The public zone (3 m +) is the zone where we want to keep people at a distance.

When attending a meeting where only a few people know you, remember that you present yourself from the moment you enter the reception until you reach the meeting room. Here are some simple tips to help you get engaged and energetic. Walk with your head as if it were a string to the North Star, and walk with energetic steps. Always show interest in those you meet, and be prepared for 'small talk'. When you are in the meeting room or similar, find a suitable place. Do not take the seat at the end of a table, it almost always indicates the position of power in the meeting room. Wait to say something until others have expressed the purpose of the meeting. Do not try to sell your ideas immediately. Wait for the right opportunity, but get involved quickly in the dialogue that takes place. When speaking, use eye contact, lean forward and speak clearly, and listen actively. It will almost without exception be appropriate to seek win–win solutions. However, you should be aware that there may be hidden agendas. These are difficult to see through, but can be brought to light by seeking to clarify misunderstandings immediately. In this way, you ensure that you or others are not overwhelmed by these hidden agendas.

If you are being confronted verbally, then there are some simple techniques, which can help you in the situation. Breathe discreetly sometimes. As you do this, show that you are actively listening. You can emphasize this by noting some of what is said. Then ask the other person to elaborate on a point, which you did not quite get, and write this down. The point is to get the other person to elaborate on what he thinks, not even if you understood his objection in the first place, because this gives you time to calm down the situation. In this way, you have already taken control of the situation. You have shown everyone that you take criticism seriously, at the same time as you have time to sum up after the verbal attack. When answering, speak calmly, slowly and clearly and in a relatively low voice. Bring out two or at most three points to the critic, where you thank him for useful advice. Then take the opportunity to emphasize your true opinion. In this way, you take the sting out of the criticism while maintaining focus on what was your real message.

In any assembly, meeting or the like, there will always be someone who is totally uninterested in what you have to convey. You can see them for yourself. They are without empathy and without expression. They seem cold and indifferent. If they get involved, then they are, as a general rule, critical. It is up to you to change your attitude. The main thesis is that you can only change others by changing your own behaviour in relation to their attitudes. Specifically, this means that you are showing these people special interest. You actively listen to what they say. If they do not express themselves, then you specifically address them and ask for their opinion. You should be especially positive towards these people, and show them respect in every way. When you have the opportunity, you should bring these people into the dialogue.

When the meeting or similar is to end, there is something you should not do. Do not unpack while someone is still talking, and do not look at the clock. This only signals that you really want to get away from there as soon as possible.

When the meeting is over, you should quickly move on to a more personal style. Re-establish consensus as soon as possible, and especially with the person or persons from whom you may have received criticism. If you leave the meeting without speaking to your critics, you should quickly establish contact with them. You should do this both to learn in more detail what the criticism was really about, and also so that the criticism does not attach itself to a picture of yourself. A golden rule is to always take one or the other hand in hand when you leave the meeting. This restores harmony and makes it easier to establish the relationship at the next meeting. Try not to be the first to leave the meeting. This only signals that you have actually been waiting a long time to get away from this meeting. If this is the case, you should after each meeting go through the ones you want to strengthen the contact with, and then send them an e-mail where you emphasize your gratitude or the like.

In general, we can say that your attitude in meetings should include the following components:

- You should show respect for age
- You should show respect for cultural differences
- You should work actively to make others feel better than they feel
- Always make sure that the other person retains dignity during and after the meeting
- Always help visitors
- Show that you care.

Now you should list three things that you want others to be left with as their impression of you. This is your personal reputation identity (POI).

1. --
2. --
3. --

In order for the other person or persons to be left with the impression you want, it is important that you demonstrate understanding of the other person or persons. Being understood seems to be a basic characteristic of any relationship and communication. Therefore, you should always have this size as a backdrop when you enter a communication situation.

Exercises

1. Think of a situation in the workplace where you meet a person for the first time, which you know you will have a lot to do with in the future.
   a. Name three things about yourself that you will try to point out to this person in your first encounter with him.
   b. Name three things about yourself that you do not want to show to this person in your first meeting.
   c. Reflect on how you think you are perceived by others. Then get help from a person who knows you relatively well to correct your own self-image.
2. Now list, after going through a-c, three things that you want to be the impression you want others to be left with after meeting you, and that you want to be lasting over time.

   List four points that you can use to get attention when selling an idea or an argument.

3. List four points that you think are important to give the individual attention, when he or she is going to sell an argument or an idea to you.
4. Think of a situation where you would convince someone of an argument or an idea you had.
   a. What feelings did you want the other person to be left with when you finished?
   b. When you think about the event in retrospect, how would you have proceeded now?
   c. How exactly could you have demonstrated understanding with the other person or people in the situation?
5. Think through your own way of representing the world. What is your main pattern: Visually, verbally, emotions, smells, tastes?
6. Think of something that you believe in, without the slightest doubt attached to it. How do you imagine this? Is it verbal, in rumours, in metaphors or the like? The answer says something about how you represent the outside world.
7. Think of a situation where you felt that you mastered the situation, i.e. where you had a positive feeling of completing the task you were to perform.
   A. Now develop a picture in your imaginary world of this situation.
      i. make this image larger.
      ii. put colours on the image.
      iii. make an inner film about this situation
      iv. put sound, emotion, smell and taste to different situations in this inner theatre.
      v. When you do this, what is the easiest thing for you to do, pictures, sound, emotions, taste, smell or the like? The easiest thing for you is probably where you have your strength in representing the outside world.
8. Now spend two to three hours walking around listening to what people are saying. Place yourself in a place where you can hear what people are saying clearly and distinctly, for example in a cafe, a restaurant, a bench in a park, etc. Listen to the following:
   a. Do they use pictures when talking?
   b. How do they use images, as metaphors, as analogies or what?
   c. How do they connect emotions to the words, by the tone of voice, by the body language or the like?
   d. Do they use a verbal language, where the sound of the words is important?
   e. How do they use the words to emphasize the verbal?
   f. How do they use the tone of voice and body language to promote the words?
   g. Write down how they represent the outside world: visually, auditory, tactile (emotions) or the like.
9. Imagine giving a talk to an assembly that is critical of you. Imagine a large aggressive dog that is your friend and facing the assembly. Imagine further that you are on a mountain top and the congregation is down in the valley. Between you lies the dog and takes care of you. After this, try to imagine the lecture again. If the dog was their friend and the congregation was on the

mountain top and you were in the valley talking to them, would you imagine the lecture differently then? If that what the dog Pluto in Donald Duck and the congregation looked like an assembly with Donalder, would this performance have changed anything for you if you were to give the talk?

Personal Communication Coaching Tools: Creative Strategy

Explanation of creative strategy.

What is creative strategy? It is a strategy to develop your dreams and give them the opportunity to be realized. Creative strategy distinguishes three vital roles when a dream is to be transformed into reality:

- The dreamer;
- The Realist and
- The critic.

This is also called Walt Disney's creative strategy. Creative strategy can be used when you want to promote creativity in yourself or in others, or when you want to test a negotiation site, for example. Creative strategy can also be used when developing new ideas in a negotiation context. You can consciously let the three roles, the dreamer, the critic and the realist take turns with people in a group you work closely with or use them yourself. If you use this technique alone, use the three roles in succession. You complete one role first, then the next and finally the third role. You start with the dreamer, because this brings out all the wild ideas that otherwise would not see the light of day. Then let the critic speak. Finally, the realist emerges. This is how you can continue by letting the dreamer go, then the critic, etc.

Exercise

Imagine a negotiation situation where you have a very specific goal you want to get through. Be as creative as possible in relation to all possible obstacles that may stand in the way of the goal being realized. Write down all the obstacles you can think of. Transform the obstacles so that you organize them according to difficulty and importance. Set up easy and important obstacles first, then set up some difficult and important and then some easy and important. This approach will motivate you through achieving results, and the effort will increase over time.

Now be the critic and ask yourself the question: What is possible to overcome these obstacles? Should I secure myself in any way? Should I have alternative strategies ready? Then put on the role of the realist, and evaluate the critic against the dreamer. List the arguments that can be put forward so that the dreamer has the opportunity to make the dreams come true. Then go another round with the dreamer, critic and realist and finally reconsider the whole negotiation situation.

References

Amen, D.G. (1998). Change your brain, change your life, Three River Press, New York.

Ashby, W.R. (1956). Introduction to cybernetics, Chapman & hall, London.

Balzer, W.K.; Doherty, M.E. & O´Connor, R.O. (1989). The effect of cognitive feedback on performance, Psychological Bulletin, 106: 410–433.

Bandura, A. (1977). Self-efficacy: Toward a unifying theory of behavioral change, Psychological Review, 84: 191–215.

Bandura, A. (1997). Self-efficacy: The exercise of control, Freeman, New York.

Bateson, G. (1972). Steps to an ecology of mind,

Bohner, G. & Wanke, M. (2002). Attitudes and attitude change, Psychology Press, London.

Collins, J.C. (2000). Good to great, harper Business, New York.

Cooper, R.K. (2001). The other 90%, Three River press, New York.

Cooper, R.K. (2006). Get out of your own way, Crown Business, New York.

Csikszentmihalyi, M. (2002). Flow, Rider, London.

Damasio, A.R. (1995). Descartes error: Emotion, reason, and the human brain, Avon, New York.

Dawes, R.M. (2001). Everyday irationality: How pseudo-scientists, lunatics, and the rest of us systematically fail to think rationally, Westview press, Boulder.

Bono, De E. (1980). Future positive thinking, Temple Smith, New York.

De Bono, E. (1991). I am right, you are wrong, Penguin, London.

De Bono, E. (2000). New thinking for the new millenium, Penguin Books, New York.

Dicintio, M.J. & Gee, S. (1999). Control is the key: Unlocking the motivation of at-risk students, Psychology in the Schools, 36: 231–237.

Drucker, P.F. (2005). Managing yourself, Harvard Business Review, jan, I harvard Business School, On Print Collection, produkt nr. 8762, s. 3–16.

Dweck, C.S. (1999). Self-theories: Their role in motivation, personality and development, Psychology Press, Philadelphia.

Early, C.P.; Northcraft, G.B.; Lee, C. & lituchy, T.R. (1990). Impact of process and outcome feedback on the relation of goalsetting to task performance, Academy of management Journal, 33: 87–105.

Ellis, A. (1979). Reason and emotion in psychoterapy, Stuart, New York.

Frankl, V.F. (1963). Man´s search for meaning, pocket books, New York.

Freeman, W.J. (1999). How brains make up their minds, Phoenix, London.

Geary, D.C. (1998). Male, female: The evolution of human sex difference, American Psychological Association, Washington, D.C.

Gelb, M.J. (1999). The how to think like leonardo da Vinci workbook, A Dell Trade paperback, New York.

Gleick, J. (1999). Faster, Pantheony, New York.

Goleman, D. (1995). Emotional intelligence, Bantam New York.

Goleman, D. (1998). Working with emotional intelligence, Bantam, New York.

Hammond, J.S.; keeney, R.L. & Raiffa, H. (1999). Smart choices: A practical guide to making better decisions, harvard Business School Press, Boston.

Hiroto, D.S. (1974). Locus of control and learned helplessness, Journal of Experimental psychology, 102: 187–193.

Johannessen, J-A. (2018). Knowledge Management as a strategic asset, Emerald, London.

Johannessen, J-A. (2018a). The future of work, Routledge, London.

Johannessen, J-A. (2019). The emergence of the fourth industrial revolution, Emerald, London.

Johannessen, J-A. (2019a). Leadership and organization in the innovation economy, Emerald, London.

Johannessen, J-A. (2019b). Automation, innovation and the end of the middle class, Routledge

Johannessen, J-A. (2020). Knowledge management for leadership and communication: AI, innovation and the digital economy, Emerald, London.

Johannessen, J-A. (2020a). Knowledge management philosophy: Communication as a strategic asset in knowledge management, Emerald, London.

Johannessen, J-A. (2020b). Automation, innovation and economic crises: Survival the fourth industrial revolution, Routledge, London.

Johannessen, J-A. (2020c). Artificial intelligence, automation and the future of competence at work, Routledge.

Johannessen, J-A. (2021). Communication as social theory, Emerald, London.

Johannessen, J-A. (2021a). Continous change and communication, Emerald, London.

Johannessen, J-A. (2021b). Artificial intelligence, automation and ethics, Routledge, London.

Johannessen, J-A. (2022). A systemic approach to continuous change in the innovation economy, Routledge, London.

Johannessen, J-A. (2022a). The philosophy of tacit knowledge, Emerald, London

Kelley, R.E. (1997). Be a star at work, Times Books, New York.

Klein, G. (1998). Sources of power: How people make decisions, MIT press, Cambridge, MA.

Klein, G. (2003). The power of intuition, Currency Doubleday, New York.

Kreiman, G.; Koch,C. & Fried,I. (2000). Imagery nevrons in the human brain, Nature, 408: 357–361.

Luhman, N. (1995). Social systems,

Maddux, J. (2005). Self-efficacy: The power of believing you can, I Snyder, C.R. & Lopez, S.J. (Red.). handbook of positive psychology, Oxford University press, Oxford, s. 277–287.

Maltz, M. (2005). The new psycho-cybernetics, Souvenir Press, New York.

Maier, S.F. & Seligman, M. (1976). Learned helplessness: Theory and evidence, Journal of Experimental Psychology, 105: 3–46.

Masten, A.S. & Reed, M-G.J. (2005). Resilience in development, I Snyder, C.R. & Lopez, S.J. (Red.). Handbook of positive psychology, Oxford University Press, Oxford.

Mednick, S.A. (1962). The associative basis of the creative process, Psychological review, 69: 220–232.

Michalko, M. (1991). Thinking toys: Handbook of business creativity, Ten Speed Press, Berkeley, Cal.

Michalko, M. (2001). Craching creativity, Ten Speed Press, Berkeley, Cal.

Parkes, K.R. (1989). Personal control in an occupational context, I Steptoe, A. & Appels, A. (Red.). Stress, personal control and health, John Wiley. London, s. 21–47.

Rossi, E.L. (1991). The twenty minute break, Tacher-Putnam, New York.

Russo, J.E. & Shoemaker, P.J.H. (1989). Decision traps: Teten barriers to brilliant decision making, Doubleday, Garden City, NY.

Ryback, D. (1998). Putting emotional intelligence to work: Succesful leadership is more than IQ, Batterworth-Heineman, Boston.

Schilling, D. (1996). Fifty activities for teaching emotional intelligence: level 1: Elemenary, Innerchoice Publishing, Torrance, CA.

Schwartz, B. (2004). The paradox of choice, Harper Collins, New York.

Seligman, M.E.P. (2006). Learned optimism, Vintage Books, New York.

Simon, H.A. (1955). A behavioral modell of rational choice, Quarterly Journal of Economics, 69: 99–118.

Simon, H.A. (1956). Rational choice and the structure of the environment, Psychological Review, 63: 129–138.

Simonton, D.K. (1999). Creativity and genius, I Pervin, L. & John, O. (Red.). Handbook of personality theory and research, Guilford, New York, s. 629–652.

Simonton, D.K. (2005). Creativity, I Snyder, C.R. & Lopez, S.J. (Red.). Handbook of positive psychology, Oxford University Press, s. 189–201.

Thompson, S.C. (1981). Will it hurt less if I can control it? Psychological Bulletin, 90: 89–101.

Thompson, S.C. (1991). The search for meaning following a stroke, basic and Applied Social Psychology, 12: 81–96.

Thompson, S.C (2005). The role of personal control in adaptive functioning, I Snyder, C. & Lopez, S.J. (Red.). Handbook of positive psychology, Oxford University press, Oxford.

Thompson, S.C; Sobolew- Shubin, A.; Galbraith, M.E.; Schwankovsky, L. & Cruzen, D. (1993). Maintaining perceptions of control: Finding perceived control in low-control circumstances, Journal of personality and Social psychology, 64: 293–304.

Weick, K. 81995). Sensemaking in organizations, Sage Publication, Thousand Oaks, CA.

Weiner, B. Frieze, I.; Kukla, A; Reed, L; Rest, S. & Rosenbaum, R.M. (1991). Perceiving the causes of success and failure, General Learning Press, Morristown, N.J.

Explanation of Concepts

25

Butterfly effect

The butterfly effect is when small variables can lead to large consequences for social systems or in the physical world.

Circular causality

Linear causal explanations are usually contrasted with teleological explanations. Linear causal explanations are usually linked to the past, while teleological explanations are linked to the future. In circular causal explanations, this distinction is eliminated and is part of a holistic integrated model, where cause, effect and expectation are viewed in context. All three elements are part of circular causal explanations. Only the relationship between cause and effect is of a linear type. If the feedback between cause and effect is introduced into the relationship, then this represents a classic cybernetic structure. When expectation is integrated into the structure, we will then have introduced a feedforward mechanism, in which the entire structure may be regarded in relation to circular causality.

Circular thinking

The main concepts in circular thinking are: feedback, feedforward, loops, loop polarity, loop dominance and compensating feedback. Circular thinking is based on circular causality.

Communicative fallacy

In an ongoing communication situation between two parties, it is not only difficult to point out what is the cause and effect of a particular part of the process, but it is also meaningless. However, this is often done by one or more of the parties in a communication situation, with the aim of putting themselves in a better light. For example, 'I said it because you said …' and so on. One party breaks up the

K. Ledingham et al., *Rethinking Innovation*,
https://doi.org/10.1007/978-3-031-40848-9_25

communication process in such a way that puts his / her own statements in a better light. But this is to compare an information and communication process with a physical process, where object A causes object B to move. This is what we can term a classic communication error, which often ends up in major conflicts, on personal or global levels, such as marital quarrels or the arms race.

Compensating feedback
An intention that is turned into an action within a system does not achieve the desired result, because external and internal responses (from the system) act in the opposite direction to the original action.

Complementary relationship
The behaviour of participant B complements the behaviour of participant A. A complementary relationship is based on basic trust and the participants having a helping attitude towards each other.

Concrete fallacy
To claim that social facts as they appear in our consciousness are concrete and objective is to succumb to the concrete fallacy, because social facts are always subjectively interpreted by an observer.

Context
The psychological framework that provides guidance for an action.

Cybernetics
In an organizational context, we distinguish between first-order, second-order and third-order cybernetics.

First-order cybernetics
First-order cybernetics concerns the control and communication in the system being controlled.

Second-order cybernetics
In second-order cybernetics, we are interested in two issues. Firstly, how the way of thinking, the language and models used by the person(s) managing an organization influence the operation of the organization. Secondly, we are interested in how the organization as a whole can learn in relation to the goals and results that emerge. In other words, second-order cybernetics focuses on organizational learning not individual learning.

Third-order cybernetics
Third-order cybernetics is concerned with the relationships and interactions between two or more observers of a social system.

Data
Data is the plural of datum, and is understood here as a set of terms, characters or symbols that in themselves do not necessarily have any meaning, but which are

represented in some type of code. In order for the data to become information, the code must be understood by an interpreter.

Displaced error

If we wish to explain a communication process, it is not sufficient to consider the individual components separately that the process consists of, and then summarize the results. The explanation must be based on considering the whole system of communication; generally, the result will be quite different from the sum of the individual results (Bunge, 1997a: 414).

The opposite approach, in which one summarizes the individual parts in order to reach a final result, may be understood as a 'displaced error'.

Distinction

A category that is used when we are considering a problem / phenomenon. The distinction is the difference that emerges when we separate two aspects of a phenomenon. For instance, model and reality, map and terrain, experience and what is experienced, the description and the described.

Feedback

The return of information.

Feedforward

This is an anticipatory mechanism, which is built into social systems, where the desire for a future state affects actions in the present.

Hidden knowledge

Hidden knowledge is here defined as the type of knowledge that structures our way of thinking and which we are not aware of.

Information

Information is here defined as the interpretation of *data*, where the code is known to the interpreter.

Information overload

A person receives more information than they can handle at any given time. This can result in the following: incompletion of tasks, errors, queue formation, filtering information which should not be filtered, abstracting where it is not appropriate, overloading of short-term memory, fleeing from situations and mixing information. Each of these factors will result in reduced efficiency in information processing.

Ithaca Syndrome

It is the process that is important, not the result.

Linear thinking

Linear thinking focuses on cause and effect where the effect comes after the cause.

Linear causality
Refer to circular causality.

Loop dominance
When positive and negative feedback loops operate, one or the other loop will dominate the social system for certain periods.

Loop polarity
In a social system, positive and negative feedback loops will always be operating.

Message
A message may be understood as consisting of three components. First, is the information component, which is what one wants to convey to the other party. Second, the message consists of a relational component, which says something about the relationship we have with the person(s) we are communicating with. Third, the message also consists of a hierarchical component, which says something about the social status of the parties in the communication situation. In order to fully interpret a message, it is therefore important that we are aware of all three components of a message.

Negative feedback
If information is returned in such a way that it decreases the deviation from a set target.

Positive feedback
When information is fed back in such a way that the deviation from the set goals is amplified.

'Protestant character'
The Protestant character has a great capacity for generating trust and authority. The character traits of this type of person are as follows: He (because the person is usually male), is a serious person, who does not smile in serious situations. For people with a Protestant character, most situations are serious. He embodies impartiality, and distances himself as a general rule from the situation at hand. He observes, but seldom shows his feelings about a situation. You will seldom or never hear him utter an ironic comment, and laughter is almost sinful. He is reasonably well-informed about most things, and as a rule expresses his opinions with a serious expression. He expresses opinions only about his own field, and then with carefully balanced consideration. He supports fairness for all, but keeps his private life separate from this. His self-image is irreproachable, and he makes a convincing case for both sides of the argument, but as a rule comes to a conclusion that benefits his own side. The Protestant character promotes trust, and is something we want to see in our public servants.

Research findings indicate that what we describe as 'the Protestant character' is not well-suited to conflict resolution. The explanation may be that even if we apparently have trust in people who possess these character traits, then there is an impression of manipulative behaviour that is implicitly present in the Protestant character.

The paradox is possibly that we have trust in the Protestant character, but we feel slightly uneasy in its presence, because in its immediate presence we notice the grasping for control, the manipulative force and the judgemental attitude to our own natures.

In other words, the Protestant character conveys a dual message: One is trust. The other is an implied force that is used as a domination technique, a kind of brutal suppression of others' spontaneity, diversity and emotional expression.

'Sauna communicative syndrome'

A feeling of freedom in social interaction is often dependent on us knowing something about the other person's position in the social hierarchy. In order to establish the position of the other person, we partake in what we can call the 'sauna communicative syndrome'. That is, in the opening gambits in conversations between two people who do not know each other, they often follow a sequence whereby each one metaphorically undresses the other, by requiring him to give his name, before quickly moving on to what the other does, i.e. his work, position and so on. What is of interest in these opening conversational gambits is not who you are, but where you fit within the social hierarchy. And if another person does not 'undress' us, then we quickly undress ourselves, even if only through a well-placed half-sentence. In this way, we become free to know what we can talk about. In the armed forces, the problem is solved by having stars on the shoulders of uniforms (the number of stars showing the rank). However, in civil life, we have to resort to other means to identify the social position of others. Consequently, we must conduct a so-called 'sauna manoeuvre', and when the social 'undressing' is finished, the conversation can start, as then we know what we can talk about, and most importantly, what we shouldn't talk about.

Sociological laws

The extent to which the social sciences, and specifically the study of communication, have laws (scientific laws) depends on whether one has a restrictive or open interpretation of what a sociological law is. If we make a distinction in social science data between intention and behaviour, we can say that intention can be understood, while behaviour can be explained. In relation to behavioural explanations, sociological laws can be created, although these cannot explain everything that happens.

A pattern may be viewed as being made up of variables that are stable over a specific period of time. A sociological law is created by an observer who gains insight into a pattern.

By acquiring insight into a pattern of social behaviour, we may also have the possibility of predicting parts of the behaviour—at least in estimated terms within a short-term perspective. Sociological laws are further linked to specific societies in time and space. The connection to time and space also applies to physical laws, although these have a longer time perspective and are more general than sociological laws.

Symmetrical relationship
In a symmetrical relationship, the behaviour of individuals is identical, and can be either positive or negative. For instance, a negative symmetrical relationship can refer to a relationship characterized by competition and mutual distrust.

System
Elements with relationships to each other and a boundary to other systems.

Systemic
The parts and the whole are viewed in relation to each other.

Systemic knowledge
In-depth knowledge (specialist), breadth- (generalist) and interrelational knowledge constitute an organization's systemic knowledge, i.e. the knowledge that considers the parts and the whole in relation to each other.

System theory
Focus on information, goals, control, change and learning in social systems. System theory is based on the fact that the world is composed of systems that interact with each other. System theory is based on insights from several disciplines. There are many different system theories.

Tacit knowledge
Tacit knowledge is the type of knowledge related to our skills that it is difficult to convey to others by using language; for instance, teaching someone how to ride a bicycle.

Thomas theorem
If a situation is defined as real, it will be real in its consequences.

Win-lose situation
Win-lose situations occur when a situation is organized in such a way that when one party 'wins', then the other party must lose.

Win–win situations
Win–win situations arise when a situation is organized in such a way that both parties gain benefits by participating in a communication process.

References

Amabile, T. (1988). A model of creativity and innovation in organizations, in Staw, B.M. & Cummings, L.L. (ed.), Research in Organizational Behavior, 9:123–167.

Amabile, T. (1996). Creativity in context, Westwiew Press, New York.

Armstrong, M. (2014a). Armstrong's handbook of strategic human resource management, Kogan Page, New York.

Armstrong, M. (2014b). Armstrong's handbook of human resource management practice, Kogan Page, New York.

Asplund, J. (1970). Om undran innfør samhället, Argos, Stockholm.

Bateson, G. (1972). Steps to an ecology of mind, Intertext Books, London.

Bleuer, H.; Bouri, M. & Mandada, F.C. (2017). New trends in medical and service robots, Springer, London.

Bleuer, H. & Bouri, M. (2017). New trends in medical and service robots: Assistive, surgical and educational robotics, Springer, London.

Boudon, R. (1981). The logic of social action, Routledge, London.

Boxall, P.F. & Purcell, J. (2003). Strategy and human resource management, Palgrave Macmillan, Basingstoke.

Boxall, P.F. & Purcell, J. (2010). An HRM perspective on employee participation, in Wilkinson, A.; Golan, P.J.; Marchington, M. & Lewins, D.(eds.), The Oxford handbook of participation in organizations, Oxford University Press, Oxford, s. 129–151.

Boxall, P.F.; Purcell, J. & Wright, P. (2007). Human resource management: Scope, analysis, and significance, in Boxall, P.F.; Purcell, J. & Wright, P., The Oxford handbook of human resource management, Oxford University Press, Oxford. s. 1–16.

Brockbank, W. (2013). Overview and logic, in Ulrich, D.; Brockbank, W.; Younger, J. & Ulrich, M. (eds.), Global HR competencies: Mastering competitive value from the outside in, McGraw Hill, New York. S. 3–27.

Bunge, M. (1967). Scientific research, Vol. 3, in Studies of the foundations methodology and philosophy of science, Springer Verlag, Berlin.

Bunge, M. (1974). Sense and reference, Reidel, Dordrecht.

Bunge, M. (1977). Treatise on basic philosophy. Vol. 3. Ontology I: The furniture of the world. Dordrecht, Holland: D. Reidel.

Bunge, M. (1979). A World of systems, Reidel, Dordrecht.

Bunge, M. (1983a). Exploring the world: Epistemology & methodology I, Dordrecht: Reidel.

Bunge, M. (1983b). Understanding the world: Epistemology & methodology II, Dordrecht: Reidel.

Bunge, M. (1985). Philosophy of science and technology. Part I: Epistemology & methodology III, Dordrecht: Reidel.

Bunge, M. (1989). Ethics: The good and the right, Reidel, Dordrecht.

Bunge, M. (1996). Finding philosophy in social science, Yale University Press, New Haven.

Bunge, M. (1997a). Mechanism and explanation. Philosophy of the Social Sciences 27: 410–465.

Bunge, M. (1997b). Foundations of Biophilosophy, Springer Verlag, Berlin.

Bunge, M. (1998). Philosophy of science: From problem to theory, Vol. 1, Transaction Publishers, New Jersey.

Coleman, J.S. (1990). Foundations of social theory, Harvard University Press, Belknap Press, Cambridge, MA.

Duncan, R. (1976). The Ambidextrual organization: Designing dual structures for innovation, in Kilman, R.H.; Pondy, L.R. & Slevin, D. (eds.), The management of organization, North Holland, New York. S. 167–188.

Elster, J. (1986). Rational choice, New York University Press, New York.

Elster, J. (1989). Nuts and bolts for the social sciences, Cambridge University Press, Cambridge.

Goleman, D. (1996). Emotional intelligence, Bloomsbury Publishing, New York.

Goleman, D. (2007). Social intelligence, Arrow Books, New York.

Grant, R.M. (2003). The knowledge-based view of the firm, in Faulkner, D. & Campell, A. (red.). The Oxford handbook of strategy, Oxford University Press, Oxford. S. 203–231.

Hamel, G. (2002). Leading the revolution: How to thrive in turbulent times by making innovation a way of life, Harvard Business School Press, Boston.

Hamel, G. (2012). What matters now: How to win in a world of relentless change ferocious competition, and unstoppable innovation, Wiley, New York.

Hamel, G. & Prahalad, C.K. (1996). Competing for the future, Harvard Business School Press, Boston.

Hedstrøm, P. & Swedberg, S.R. (1998). Social mechanisms: An introductory essay, in Hedstrøm, P. & R. Swedberg (red.), Social mechanisms: An analytical approach to social theory, Cambridge University Press, Cambridge. Pp. 20–32.

Helfat, C. E.; Finkelstein, S.; Mitchell, W.; Peteraf, M.A.; Singh, H.; Teece, D.J. & Winter, S.G. (2007). Dynamic capabilities: Understanding strategic change in organizations, Blackwell, Oxford.

Hernes, G. (1998). Real virtuality, in social mechanisms: An analytical approach to social theory, edited by Peter Hedstrøm and Richard Swedberg, Cambridge University Press, Cambridge. Pp. 74–102.

Hewing, M. (2013). Collaboration with potential users for discontinuous innovation, Springer Gabler, Potsdam.

Johannessen, J.-A. (1996). Systemics applied to the study of organizational fields: Developing systemic research strategy for organizational fields, Kybernetes, 25, 1: 33–51.

Johannessen, J.-A. (1997). Aspects of ethics in systemic thinking, Kybernetes, 26, 9: 983–1001.

Johannessen, J.-A. (2018). Innovation leads to economic crises, Palgrave, London.

Johannessen, J.-A. (2020a). The workplace of the future, Routledge, London.

Johannessen, J.-A. (2020b). Automation, innovation and economic crises: Survival the fourth industrial revolution, Routledge, London.

Johannessen, J.-A. (2020c). Artificial intelligence, automation and the future of competence at work, Routledge.

Johannessen, J.-A. (2020d). Knowledge management for leadership and communication: AI, innovation and the digital economy, Emerald, London.

Johannessen, J.-A. (2020e). Knowledge management philosophy: Communication as a strategic asset in knowledge management, Emerald, London.

Johannessen, J.-A. (2021a). China's innovation economy: Artificial intelligence and the new silk road, Routledge, London.

Johannessen, J.-A. (2021b). Artificial intelligence, automation and ethics in the innovation economy, Routledge, London.

Johannessen, J.-A. (2021c). Communication as social theory: The social side of knowledge management, Emerald, London.

Johannessen, J.-A. (2022a). Creativity, innovation and the fourth industrial revolution:
The da Vinci strategy, Routledge, London.

Johannessen, J.-A. (2022b). The new silk road and the innovation economy in China, Routledge, London.

Johannessen, J.-A. (2022c). The philosophy of tacit knowledge, Emerald, London.

Johannessen, J.-A. (2022d). A systemic approach to continuous change in the innovation economy, Routledge, London.

Johannessen, J.-A. (2022e). Intelligent robots consciousness and creativity: The search for hidden knowledge, The cognitive side of knowledge management, Emerald, London.

Johannessen, J.-A. (2023a). A Marxist interpretation of Chuch leadership: Romans: 13: 1–7, Lexington Books, New York.

Johannessen, J.-A. (2023b). Feudalcapitalism: The political economy of the innovation society, Routledge, London.

Johannessen, J.-A. (2023c). De-globalization, China-US tensions in the Innovation Economy, Routledge, London.

Johannessen, J.-A. (2023d). Artificial intelligence and creativity: Implications for automation in the innovation economy, Routledge, London.

Johannessen, J.-A. (2023e). The fourth industrial revolution and the labor market: Future proofing work in the innovation economy, Routledge, London.

Johannessen, J.-A. (2023f). Aspects of a theory of Genocide, Trivent Publishing, London.

Johannessen, J.-A.; Olaisen, J. & Olsen, B. (2001). Mismanagement of tacit knowledge: The importance of tacit knowledge, the danger of information technology, and what to do about it? International Journal of Information Management, 21, 3: 3–20.

Johannessen, J.-A. & Olaisen, J. (2005). Systemic philosophy and the philosophy of social science-Part I: Transcedence of the naturalistic and the anti-naturalistic position in the philosophy of social science, Kybernetes 34, 7/8: 1261–1277.

Johannessen, J.-A. & Olaisen, J. (2006). Systemic philosophy and the philosophy of social science-Part II: The systemic position, Kybernetes 34, 9/10: 1570–1586.

Kirzner, S. (1982). The theory of entrepreneurship in economic growth, in Kent, C.A.; Sexton, D. L. & Vesper, K.H. (red.), Encyclopedia of entrepreneurship, Prentice Hall, Englewood Cliffs, N.J.

Merton, R.K. (1967). Social theory and social structure, Free Press, London.

Mosco, V. & McKercher, C. (2007). Introduction: Theorizing knowledge labor and the information society. Knowledge workers in the information society, Lexington Books, Lanham.

Miller, J.G. (1978). Living systems, McGraw-Hill, New York.

Nelson, R.R. & Winter, S.G. (1982). An evolutionary theory of economic change, Harvard University Press, Cambridge, MA.

North, D.C. (1990). Institutions, institutional change and economic performance, Cambridge University Press, Cambridge.

North, D.C. (1993). Nobel lecture: http://www.nobelprize.org/nobel_prizes/economics/laureates/1993/north-lecture.html#not2, lesedato, 4.5.2012.

OECD (2000a). A New Economy? The changing role of innovation and information technology in growth, Paris.

OECD (2000b). Economic Outlook, Paris.

OECD (2000c). Education at a Glance: OECD Indicators, CERI, Paris.

OECD (2000d). ICT Skills and Employment, Working party on the information economy, Paris, 15 November, DSTI/ICCP/IE (2000)7.

OECD (2000e). Knowledge Management in the Learning Society, CERI, Paris.

OECD (2001). Innovative clusters: Driving of national innovation-systems, OECD, Paris.

O'Reilly, C.A. & Tushman, M.L. (2004). The ambidextrous organization, Harvard Business Review, 82, 4: 74–81.

O'Reilly, C.A. & Tushman, M.L. (2007). Ambidexterity as a dynamic capability: Resolving the innovators dilemma, Harvard Business School Press, Boston.

O'Reilly, C.A. & Tushman, M.L. (2011). Organizational ambidexterity in action: How managers explore and exploit, California Management Review, 53, 4: 5–22.

Reinhardt, W., Smith, B.; Sloep, P. & Drachler, H. (2011). Knowledge worker roles and Actions–Results of two empirical studies, Knowledge and Process Management 18, 3: 150–174.

Roddick, D.A. (2003). The grassroots entrepreneur, in Elbæk, U. Kaospilot A-Z, Narayana Press, Gylling.

Stone, J. (1979). The revival of narrative: Reflections on a new old history, Past and Present, 85: 3–24.

Storey, J.; Ulrich, D. & Wright, P.M. (2009). Introduction, in Storey, J.; Wright, P.M. & Ulrich, D. (ed.), The Routledge companion to strategic human resource management, Routledge, London. Pp. 3–15.

Teece, D.J. (2013). Dynamic Capabilities and Strategic management: Organizing for Innovation, OUP, Oxford.

Teece, D.; Pisano, G. & Shuen, A. (1997). Dynamic capabilities and strategic management, Strategic Management Journal, 18, 7: 509–533.

Thota, H. & Munir, Z. (2011). Key concepts in innovation, Palgrave Macmillan, London.

Tushman, M.L. & O'Reilly, C.A. (1996). Ambidextrous organization: Managing Torrington et al., 2005.

Ulrich, D. (2013). Foreword, in Ulrich, D.; Brockbank, W.; Younger, J. & Ulrich, M. (eds.), Global HR competencies: Mastering competitive value from the outside in, McGraw Hill, New York. S. v–xxi.

Ulrich, D. (2013a). Future of global HR: What's next?, in Ulrich, D.; Brockbank, W.; Younger, J. & Ulrich, M. (eds.), Global HR competencies: Mastering competitive value from the outside in, McGraw Hill, New York. Pp. 255–268.

Ulrich, D. & Brockbank, W. (2005). The HR value proposition, Harvard Business School Press, Boston, MA.

Vadakkepat, P. & Goswami, P. (eds.). (2018). Humanoid robotics: A reference, Springer, London.

Wang, Q-G.; Lee, T.H. & Lin, C. (2003). Relay feedback: Analysis, identification and control, Springer, London.

Wernerfelt, B. (1984). A resource-based view of the firm, Strategic Management Journal, 5, 2: 171–180.

White, J. & Younger, J. (2013). The global perspective, in Ulrich, D.; Brockbank, W.; Younger, J. & Ulrich, M. (eds.), Global HR competencies: Mastering competitive value from the outside in, McGraw Hill, New York. Pp. 27–53.

Wilson, M. (2017). Implementation of robot systems, Butterworth-Heinemann, New York.

Winfield, A. (2012). Robotics, OUP, Oxford.

Wright, P.M.; Boudreau, J.W.; Pace, D.A.; Libby Sartain, E.; McKinnon, P. & Antoine, R.L. (eds.). (2011). The chief HR officer: Defining the new role of human resource leaders, Jossey-Bass, London.

Wright, P.; Dunford, B. & Snell, S. (2001). Human resources and the resource based view of the firm, Journal of Management, 27: 701–721.

Winter, S.G. (2003). Understanding dynamic capabilities, Strategic Management Journal, 24: 991–995.

Zaltman, G.; Duncan, R. & Holbeck, J. (1973). Innovations and organizations, Wiley, New York.

Index

K. Ledingham et al., *Rethinking Innovation*, https://doi.org/10.1007/978-3-031-40848-9

Made in the USA
Monee, IL
13 September 2026

62973715R00122